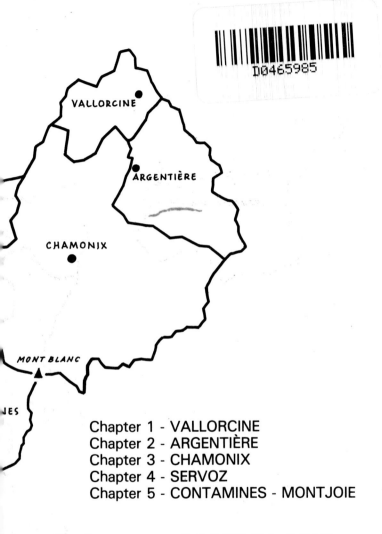

Chapter 1 - VALLORCINE
Chapter 2 - ARGENTIÈRE
Chapter 3 - CHAMONIX
Chapter 4 - SERVOZ
Chapter 5 - CONTAMINES - MONTJOIE

# CHAMONIX - MONT-BLANC

# CHAMONIX-MONT-BLANC

*Mer de Glace (centre right) and surrounding peaks from the
Grand Balcon Sud trail (Walk 11)*

# CHAMONIX-MONT-BLANC
## A WALKING GUIDE

by

**Martin Collins**

CICERONE PRESS

© Martin Collins 1988
Published by Cicerone Press, 2 Police Square,
Milnthorpe, Cumbria, England

First published 1988
Reprinted 1992, 1998

ISBN 1 85284 009 9

Other guide books for walkers, in this series, include:
*The Tour of Mont Blanc - Andrew Harper*
*Walking the French Alps (GR5) - Martin Collins*
*Tour of the Oisans (GR54) - Andrew Harper*
*The Tour of the Queyras - Alan Castle*
*Chamonix to Zermatt, the Walker's High Level Route - Kev Reynolds*
*Alpine Pass Route, Switzterland - Kev Reynolds*
*The Bernese Alps - A Walking Guide - Kev Reynolds*
*Walks in the Engadine, Switzerland - Kev Reynolds*
*Walking in Ticino, Switzerland - Kev Reynolds*
*The Valais, Switzerland, A Walking Guide - Kev Reynolds*
*The Kalkalpen Traverse - Alan Proctor*
*Mountain Walking in Austria - Davies*
*Alta Via, High Level Walks in the Dolomites - Martin Collins*
*Walking in the Dolomites - Gillian Price*

Cicerone produce a wide range of books of interest to the outdoor enthusiast.
Please write for catalogue.

Photographs, maps, view profiles and drawings by the author.

*Front cover: Above Le Tour, Mont Blanc in the background*
*Back cover: Descending from the Brévent*

# CONTENTS

*Page*

Introduction ................................................................. 7
About the Walks ............................................................. 13
When to go and how to get there ........................................ 15
Accommodation ............................................................. 18
Main Tourist Offices ....................................................... 21
Clothing and Equipment ................................................... 21
Maps ........................................................................ 24
Mountain Safety ............................................................ 25
Weather, and obtaining a Forecast ...................................... 27
Nature Reserves, Flora and Fauna ...................................... 29
Topography and Glaciers .................................................. 31
Features encountered on the Walks ..................................... 38
CHAPTER 1 – The Vallorcine area ...................................... 41
CHAPTER 2 – The Argentière area ...................................... 69
CHAPTER 3 – The Chamonix valley ..................................... 97
CHAPTER 4 – Servoz and Plateau d'Assy .............................. 146
CHAPTER 5 – The Contamines-Montjoie valley ....................... 159
The main summer season Lifts ........................................... 190
Useful Addresses .......................................................... 191

For Diana and Paul

'I look on high;
Has some unknown omnipotence unfurled
The veil of life and death? or do I lie
In dream, and does the mightier world of sleep
Speed far around and inaccessibly
Its circles? For the very spirit fails,
Driven like a homeless cloud from steep to steep
That vanishes among the veiwless gales!
Far, far above, piercing the infinite sky,
Mont Blanc appears – still, snowy and serene.'

*Shelley (Lines from 'Mont Blanc', 1816)*

# INTRODUCTION

In the Middle Ages, mountains were the focus of ancestral terror, their high snows, ravines, rock peaks and glaciers the haunts of demons and unknown creatures. 'Oh Lord, let me live that I may warn my brethren not to come to this place of torment' prayed a Canterbury monk in 1188. Priests, soldiers and traders crossed the alpine landscape with reluctance and considerable apprehension, erecting cairns and crosses against this potent source of fear and superstition. Mont Blanc was known as 'La Mont Maudite' – 'The Accursed Mountain' – and with no scientific or philosophical rationale to support an objective view of its dramatic natural phenomena, little wonder that human beings responded with awe and foreboding.

A number of mule-tracks and footpaths in the Alpes de Savoie probably date back to pre-historic times and certainly to the Roman era, crossing such strategically and geographically important passes as Balme, Anterne, Bonhomme and Seigne. The 'Chamouni' valley was, however, rarely visited by outsiders and was scantily settled, with just one small community huddled round a monastic farm by the early 15th century. It would not be long before this isolation came to an end for good.

In 1741, an expedition of seven Englishmen, among them the experienced traveller Richard Pocock, set out under the leadership of wealthy young William Wyndham to explore Montenvers and the 'storm-lashed frozen lake' we now know as Mer de Glace. Wyndham's eloquent 'Voyages aux Glaciers de Savoie', published on his return to London, whetted the appetites of many a would-be wanderer and undoubtedly contributed to Chamonix becoming one of the world's earliest tourist destinations.

Artists, writers, philosophers, musicians and nobility joined a swelling tide of adventurers transported by horse-drawn cart and mule train up rough valley tracks to witness the great glaciers for themselves. In 1760, the naturalist Horace Bénédict de Saussure visited Chamonix, climbed Le Brévent and offered a reward for anyone who could find a way up Mont Blanc – a problem he considered insoluble. Over the next two decades many local chamois hunters and crystal gatherers would attempt the ascent, but without success.

1773 saw an intrepid Scotsman, Thomas Blaikie, making a

noteworthy walk from the Mer de Glace, past the base of the Chamonix Aiguilles and the Blaitière chalets, traversing the Bossons Glacier, Montagne de la Côte and the Taconnaz Glacier to reach the base of Aiguille du Goûter. He was guided by the young Michel-Gabriel Paccard, a name of great significance in the subsequent Mont Blanc story.

Marc-Théodore Bourrit, a Genevan cantor, frequented the Chamonix valley and became involved in early forays up Mont Blanc from several directions, his party reaching 4000m in 1784. De Saussure and Bourrit joined forces the following year, bivouacing at 2700m; Bourrit, however, developed altitude sickness and was forced to retreat.

On 8th August 1786, Dr. Michel-Gabriel Paccard and the crystal-hunter Jacques Balmat, who was already well acquainted with this high-mountain environment, finally climbed to the summit of Mont Blanc, though their heroic achievement was later tainted by squabbling and misrepresentation. De Saussure himself, along with a sizeable entourage of guides which included Jacques Balmat, repeated the ascent in 1787 in weather kind enough to allow him to conduct scientific experiments on the summit. (A full account of these events, along with a comprehensive history of Mont Blanc, are contained in Walt Unsworth's excellent book 'Savage Snows' published by Hodder and Stoughton).

At this time, the furtherance of science was still the only acceptable justification for climbing, yet there developed a parallel public adulation of Nature, a romanticism which fired the imaginations of poets and artists confronted by the barren beauty of wild places. When Shelley visited Chamonix in 1816, he found the grandeur of the Mont Blanc massif almost overwhelming: 'But how shall I describe to you the scenes by which I am now surrounded;' he wrote in a letter to Thomas Peacock. '. . . I never knew, I never imagined what mountains were before. The immensity of these aerial summits excited, when they suddenly burst upon the sight, a sentiment of ecstatic wonder not unallied to madness . . .'

By now, Chamonix-Mont-Blanc was a well established component in the European 'Grand Tour' and a tourist destination in its own right. It boasted three hotels, including the famous Hotel d'Angleterre, and English visitors outnumbered other nationals even though the journey from London took nine days.

British involvement in climbing and exploration was prominent too, epitomised by the young Scottish goelogist Professor James Forbes, who came to the Alps in 1826 and travelled the region

*Mont Blanc from the Col du Brévent*

extensively for a quarter of a century. His 'Travels Through the Alps of Savoy' and other books eventually helped bring about the popularisation of mountaineering as sport. The advent of the 'Golden Age', which saw many great summits climbed for the first time – often by British alpinists – ended with Edward Whymper's ill-fated attempt on the Matterhorn in 1865. Meanwhile, the Alpine Club, first of its kind in the world, had been founded in London in 1857 and John Ball elected as its inaugural president.

Following his visit there in 1860 to mark the incorporation of Savoie into France, Napoleon III undertook to improve road access to the Chamonix valley. Seven years later the new road had been built and with it came larger coaches and an ever greater volume of tourists, mainly English, Americans and the French themselves. Hotels and lodging houses were increasing in number and mountain guides began forming themselves into 'compagnies' to service the influx of mountain sightseers.

In 1892 a huge mudslide emanating from the Bionnassay Glacier swept down to the Contamines-Montjoie valley, obliterating Bionnay village and killing some 200 people. In the same year, plans were put forward for building a rack-and-pinion railway from Chamonix to Montenvers, amidst cries of outrage from aesthetes, alpinists and guides who saw in it an erosion of their exclusive domain

*The Tramway du Mont Blanc at Col de Voza*

and even their livelihoods. The line was officially opened in 1908, three years after Chamonix had been connected to the main French rail network, and the old mule-trains which had faithfully transported visitors for half a century finally disappeared. In the event, fears proved groundless since easier public access to Montenvers produced more work than ever for the guides and the great empty spaces of the high mountains remained largely inviolate.

A comparable venture began at the other, southern, end of the Chamonix valley when a mountain railway was conceived to run from Le Fayet to the very summit of Mont Blanc: these were not tentative years in civil engineering! Opened in 1912, the Tramway du Mont Blanc reached above the Bionnassay Glacier to Le Nid d'Aigle – its present terminus – but no further; impossibly difficult ground prevented any continuation.

Around the turn of the century, skiing had evolved, first to aid travel over soft snow on approaches to climbs and later as a competitive sport, with the first Winter Olympics being held at Chamonix in 1924. What began as a low-profile, minority sport rapidly grew fashionable and after the second World War developed into the vast seasonal winter sports industry we know today. Modest village hotels and the odd 'télépherique' constructed during the 1920's and 30's gave way to the creation of purpose-built resorts, bulldozed pistes and forests of ski-lifts, particularly over the past two or three decades.

By 1928 the writing was already on the wall. In Chamonix for a season's climbing, the great explorer and mountaineer Eric Shipton wrote: '. . . Chamonix itself is a horrible place. It combines everything ugly and vulgar in modern 'tourism'; vast hotels sprout in unsightly clusters, charabancs roar through the streets, every kind of cheapjack is there to exploit the mountains. Unfortunately these horrors of mass touristdom are not confined to the main valley. In the height of the season the mountain huts overflow with trippers, many of whom having no intention of climbing, create an intolerable hubbub which continues far into the night, and they generally leave the huts in a state of filth and disorder. Even among the climbers there is an atmosphere of fevered competition . . .'

Shipton's rather jaundiced perception of the area may have been coloured by comparison with earlier exploits in unvisited regions such as Norway and the Dauphiné. In the same year he moderated his judgement: 'The Alps for all their limitations, their sophistication, their spoiling, have some qualities that I have not found in other ranges. It is difficult to describe these qualities exactly, but they are due I fancy to tradition, to the higher culture of the native inhabitants, to the easy friendships made and to the wonderful variety of scene small enough in scale to be easily appreciated and large enough to be wholly satisfying.'

Possibly the best known and certainly the most stomach-turning ride in the valley area is the Aiguille du Midi cable-car. First proposals for a 'funicular' date back to the early years of this century but work was curtailed by the First World War, having reached Gare des Glaciers. Resurrecting the idea, an Italian engineer, Dino Lora Totino, chose a different line to the original one. Guides from Aosta and Chamonix, aided by some 30 alpinists, managed to haul a cable to the summit of Piton Nord which was eventually joined to the adjacent Piton Central by footbridge. The cable-car's first stage to Plan de l'Aiguille began operations in 1954, the spectacular second stage a year later. Given suitable weather conditions, a further aerial journey can be made high above the Vallée Blanche to Pointe Helbronner on the Italian frontier.

With the construction of the Autoroute Blanche, then in 1965 the opening of the Mont Blanc Tunnel through to Italy, Chamonix became fully 'plugged in' to the European road network. True to its resort origins, the valley's amenities have moved with the times and today's smart bars, sports complexes, apartment blocks, campsites,

*Ski-lift development at La Croix-de-Lognan*

shops and discos may seem a far cry from the simple provision available to those first curious travellers. Certainly our media-swamped perception of the world is rather less innocent! But it is surprising how quickly differences recede as you climb above the hustle and bustle into the timeless silence of the high trails.

At first sight, the Chamonix valley and its environs do not constitute true wilderness country (though you are soon alone on untrodden ground away from footpaths). During the summer season other walkers will be sharing the more popular trails with you, sustained by a network of refuges, chalet-hôtels and 'buvettes' which act as a foil to the unmanageable infinities of rock, snow and sky.

Shipton's version of Chamonix does have its modern corollary, though it is far less unpleasant than one might expect. A busy town dedicated to meeting the diverse needs of climbers, mountaineers, hikers and holidaymakers who flock here in their thousands, Chamonix still deserves a place on any would-be European 'Grand Tour'. Despite an image-conscious, competitive milieu, the place manages to retain an atmosphere of wide-eyed excitement, for steeply above rises Shelley's vision of breathtaking mountain grandeur. Mont Blanc's snowy dome, at 4807m (15,771ft) the highest point in Western Europe, is no remote summit far from the nearest habitation, but an almost tangible presence towering overhead into the southern sky and buttressed by a shining array of satellite peaks and glaciers.

The face of these mountains has undergone greater change during the last three decades than in all previous history. Ski-lifts, pistes, cable-cars and cabin-lifts, chalet development and access tracks have all conspired to scar the landscape and exacerbate erosion. For summer walkers the impact is greatest, winter's concealing snow cover having melted away.

Yet somehow the scale and beauty of this popularised corner of the Alps transcends any regret we may feel at man's feeble scratchings and apprehension for the future. It is impossible to remain unmoved by such elemental country: for all our well-beaten tracks and mechanical lifts, we still venture forth at some personal risk from objective dangers. The rewards for reaching those high places accessible only on foot will last a lifetime.

## ABOUT THE WALKS

Most outings in this guidebook are of a day's duration, though one or two would prove testing in that time and a few are rather shorter. The principal exception is Walk No. 5, a tour of the Aiguilles Rouges massif requiring 2 to 3 days to complete. Following each area chapter are suggestions for shorter walks occupying half a day or less.

The variety of routes is considerable, ranging from those over easy terrain involving only modest ascent, to strenuous climbs traversing rugged ground with scrambling and snowslopes to negotiate. On the whole, paths are well defined and the effort of prolonged ascent will usually be mollified by zig-zags which reduce the effective gradient. Waymarking is universally good.

Early in the season (mid to late June), large amounts of lying snow (névé) cover sections of paths above about 2000m (6500ft). As summer progresses, the snow gradually melts away, reaching a minimum in September before the fresh falls of autumn. Throughout the walking season, however, snow-filled gullies and stream valleys, as well as extensive snowfields which never diminish significantly, present walkers with a surface demanding care, especially above big drops.

The best known and most walked routes can become quite social affairs in peak season, fellow hikers prompting a frequent 'Bonjour' as they pass. Continentals take their sport seriously and their behaviour on the trail is both impeccable and friendly. Add to this the expansiveness of the alpine mountain scene, and there is rarely any sense of crowding once away from the valley and cable-car stations. The least frequented walks are located around Vallorcine, Plateau d'Assy and Les Contamines-Montjoie.

Many walks are comparable to a good day out in the hills of North Wales, the Lake District or the Scottish Highlands, but there are some major differences. Owing to the sheer size of the major summits and the need to avoid the soft snow conditions of mid to late daytime, climbers often start very early in the morning from refuges situated in high locations. A great advantage for mountain walkers is that these same refuges offer meals, drinks and accommodation in sensational high-mountain environments. Chalet-hôtels and 'buvettes' or 'crèmeries' (alpine snack-bars) provide much the same service at lower altitudes.

Cable-cars and cabin-lifts are used widely by walkers and climbers alike, whisking you up to around 2000m – or down – and increasing options on some routes. In the event of deteriorating weather, injury or plain fatigue, these mechanical lifts enable a retreat to be made down to the valley, provided it is during operating hours. (See 'The Main Summer-Season Lifts').

Possibly the most dramatic contrast with British hills is the constant proximity of glaciers and high snows which add a visual dimension of magnetic beauty.

*The precipitous trail below the Desert de Platé*

Each route description in this guidebook is preceded by some useful statistics:– the total amount of ascent involved, approximate timings between places (not allowing for prolonged halts for meals etc.), the availability of refreshments and accommodation, and notes pertaining to any special features or technical difficulty. Thus by checking the text first, walks can be chosen to suit most inclinations. Often your level of fitness, and particularly the prevailing weather, will dictate what it is possible to achieve on a given day.

It is always wise to go properly equipped, to obtain a weather forecast before setting out and not to overestimate your stamina and ability. Also be alert to changes in path routing caused by avalanche, landslip, storm and forestry work.

# WHEN TO GO AND HOW TO GET THERE

Winter sees substantial snowfall in the Mont Blanc area and Chamonix is transformed into a major skiing centre. What walking may be possible during this season lies outside the scope of this guidebook.

Springtime is relatively brief, lasting from about mid-May to mid-June, depending on prevailing weather cycles. Winter snows are melting and there is a real risk of avalanches, more especially during May. With heavy snow cover still obscuring the higher paths, walking is distinctly alpine in flavour, requiring winter hill-walking skills and a knowledge of snow conditions. Footbridges over glacial torrents may not yet have been installed for the summer hiking season, and meltwater will be swelling all water courses. Many refuges and mechanical lifts are closed until mid-June, so extra prudence is needed when arranging overnight accommodation.

From mid-June onwards the alpine environment breaks free of winter's grip and some of the most beautiful wild flowers to be found anywhere in Europe emblazon trails with a riot of colour. With clear, sparkling air and a generous quantity of snow still defining the higher ground, June (and often early July) are visually outstanding.

The main walking season begins in July with the onset of summer. Paths are largely snow-free, the days are long, the sun warm, although afternoon thunderstorms are more likely. Chamonix-Mont-Blanc receives its greatest influx of summer visitors during July and August. Among them will be tourist sightseers; family holidaymakers there for the fresh air, sporting amenities and entertainments; paragliders launching themselves from Planpraz and other eyries to soar over the town; backpackers on the Tour du Mont

*Early season at the Lac Blanc refuge*

Blanc or <u>GR5 Traverse of the Alps</u>; hikers, rock-climbers, alpinists and guides.

At this time, everything is open, from mountain zoos to nightclubs, cable-cars and mountain railways to refuges and 'buvettes'. Accommodation is at a premium and it is wise to book in advance if possible. The valley is buzzing with activity and popular trails are well walked, but adjacent mountains are very large indeed and, human nature being what it is, only serious walkers will reach the more rugged areas covered by this guidebook.

By the end of August the main continental holiday period is over. During the last two weeks of September and for much of October, walking will be through a landscape highlighted by golden larch forest with chill autumnal air heralding the first snowfalls of winter. Refuges and many of the valley's tourist amenities will close, but the autumn walker, in common with his spring counterpart, is likely to enjoy uniquely beautiful scenery and a greater chance of settled weather.

**Getting there by road**

Road access to Chamonix-Mont-Blanc is best gained from the

south-west on the B41 'Autoroute Blanche' which continues as the N205, rising on a long elevated section from Le Fayet. Unless you intend using the Mont Blanc Tunnel, the main road by-passing Chamonix threads up the Arve valley as the N506, passing through Argentière and crossing Col des Montets to reach Vallorcine and the Swiss frontier. Several minor roads serve the Chamonix valley villages.

Plateau d'Assy (Walks 23 and 24) lies up the D43 from Passy. The Contamines-Montjoie valley (Walks 25 to 31) is reached on the D902 from St. Gervais-les-Bains.

**Getting there by train**
The Chamonix and Vallorcine valleys are served by trains on the main French railway network (S.N.C.F.), with stations at Le Fayet, Servoz, Les Houches, Chamonix, Argentière, Montroc, Le Buet and Vallorcine. It is thus possible by enquiring at your Travel Agent or British Rail to arrange a train journey from Britain right through to the area covered by this guidebook. Advice will also be given about seat, couchette or sleeping-car reservations and any special fare concessions available. Advance booking is essential for travel during July and August.

Some long-distance services are boarded at the French channel port and taken round Paris, so that no changing is involved until the Alps are reached at Le Fayet. Other services arrive at Paris Nord, necessitating a ride across Paris to Gare de Lyon by inter-station bus. In any case, trains are numbered and have destination boards on carriages, removing any uncertainty from the process of changing.

**Getting there by air**
Geneva is the nearest international airport to Chamonix-Mont-Blanc, with scheduled services operated by British Airways and Air France leaving Heathrow and Manchester. Travel Agents will have details of these and other connecting flights. There is a coach service to Chamonix.

Tourist air circuits over the Mont Blanc massif, operated by the Compagnie Air-Mont-Blanc, depart from Sallanches.

**Public Transport in the area**
The Chamonix valley from Les Houches to Col des Montets enjoys a frequent bus service, calling at all villages and main campsites. There is also a train service (less frequent), with stations and halts right up the valley and, via the Montroc Tunnel, to Le Buet and Vallorcine.

*'La Floria', a typical mid-height buvette*

Plateau d'Assy lies on a bus route from Sallanches to Guébriant. Les Contamines connects by bus with Le Fayet and Geneva. A service also extends from Les Contamines to Notre-Dame-de-la-Gorge.

# ACCOMMODATION

### Hotels

Within the Chamonix-Mont-Blanc area there are numerous hotels, logis (smaller family establishments) and auberges (inns) of all star grades, in addition to self-catering apartments and chalets. If arriving with no prior booking, a visit to the nearest Office du Tourisme (see below) will usually yield a bed for the night. Visitors are strongly advised, however, to make hotel reservations in advance during the peak season. Unlike in Britain, you normally pay for the room, having inspected it first, and are sometimes expected to eat in the hotel restaurant. Continental breakfasts on their own will not sustain a hard morning's walking!

### Refuges

These are either privately owned or run by organisations such as Club Alpin Français or Touring Club de France. Specifications and service in refuges vary widely, being dependent on their size, location and means of access. Beds are often communally grouped in 'dortoirs', but the larger establishments will offer smaller, family-sized rooms. By no means all refuges are reached by jeep-track, some relying on cable-lifts, helicopters or even the legs of the resident guardian to bring up supplies!

In the summer season, refuges in the Mont Blanc area are extremely popular and many of the higher ones are used by alpinists and climbers too. Consequently there is considerable competition for beds and advance booking is definitely recommended, particularly for groups. Should this be impossible, try to arrive early. A sheet liner and indoor shoes (trainers or moccasins) should be carried.

Refuges are rarely peaceful places! Mountaineers tend to leave long before dawn and the sound of their preparations and departure is likely to disturb other visitors. However, for many walkers at least one night spent soaking up the unique atmosphere of a high-mountain refuge will prove a worthwhile and memorable experience.

Owing to problems of access during the snowfalls of winter, most refuges open only between mid-June and mid-September, though a few remain part-open and unmanned for winter climbers. Details of opening dates, numbers of beds, availability of meals, and telephone numbers where applicable appear in the text.

### Gîtes d'étape

Not to be confused with gîtes (rented holiday homes), gîtes d'étape are similar in concept to British youth hostels, but are less formal and do not require membership of an organisation. Sleeping arrangements are usually in 'dortoirs' with pillows and blankets provided and there will be a common-room, kitchen, toilets and bathroom. Maximum stay is three nights and some gîtes d'étape are self-catering. Booking ahead is certainly advisable in peak season, otherwise arrive early. For up-to-date prices and availability of gîtes d'étape (many are closed out of season), consult the local tourist information office.

### Camping

Camping carnets are universally required at site offices on your arrival. They offer proof of identity and third party insurance and can be obtained in Britain through such organisations as the Camping Club, Youth Hostels' Association, etc.

With few exceptions, campsites around Chamonix are well appointed and suitable for a prolonged stay. They are, however,

*The Platé Refuge*

heavily patronised by continental family groups, so booking in advance during the peak season (mid-July to mid-August) is desirable, though not essential if you are prepared to travel around in search of a vacancy. Backpackers with small tents can usually be squeezed into the busiest of sites.

Sites usually have good toilet and washing facilities, bread delivery daily, a shop or bar and helpful staff. There is an orderliness and a level of mutual consideration on French campsites not always found on British ones and it is usually possible to get a good night's sleep! You pay separately for the 'emplacement', the number of people, tents and vehicles in your party, and for connection to electricity if required.

Informal camping seems to be officially tolerated at Les Planards, rough ground near Col des Montets, but there are no facilities or security for leaving tents pitched, other than an occasional gendarme patrol. Informal camping is also found at Plaine Joux above Plateau d'Assy, but is controlled by 'Le Ranch' snack bar proprietors to whom a fee is payable.

Backpackers are much freer to pitch wild ('camping sauvage'), though this is inadvisable below about 2000m (6500ft) owing to frequent use of the valley and intermediate-height trails. Above this altitude and well away from habitations, possibilities are unlimited, many locations being of exceptional quality. Every attempt should be made to follow the backpacker's code: leave no sign of having camped, avoid fouling the environment, take litter with you and guard against starting fires in undergrowth or forest. In the Contamines-Montjoie valley above Notre-Dame-de-la-Gorge, two sites have been specifically designated for overnight lightweight campers and, in fact, this whole area lends itself more readily to backpacking than the Chamonix valley.

**The main Tourist Offices**
VALLORCINE – Syndicate d'Initiative, railway station, tel: (50)54.60.71
ARGENTIÈRE – Office du Tourisme, town centre, tel: (50)54.02.14
CHAMONIX – Office du Tourisme, Place de l'Eglise, tel: (50)50.00.24. Hotel reservations tel: (50)53.23.33.
LES HOUCHES – Office du Tourisme, town centre, tel: (50)54.40.62.
SERVOZ – Syndicat d'Initiative, tel: (50)47.21.68.
LE FAYET – Syndicat d'Initiative, tel: (50)78.13.88.
LES CONTAMINES-MONTJOIE – Office du Tourisme, town centre, tel: (50)47.01.58.

# CLOTHING AND EQUIPMENT

From any of the cable-car high stations on a fine summer's day, holidaymakers trudge off optimistically towards their chosen destination, having been spared the effort of walking up from the valley. All ages are represented and the majority are adequately equipped, but inevitably some are clad only for the ride up, unaware of any need for a different kind of clothing when perhaps 1000m (3300ft) above the valley floor. If their aim is a nearby picnic, this is of no consequence, but venturing further afield would introduce positive risks.

On the heavily snowbanked trail from Pranpraz to Lac Cornu, the author encountered a gentleman dressed in shirt, slacks and moccasins slithering precariously along the narrow ledge of trodden

*Fine early season conditions above the Chéserys lakes*

slush which passed for a path. Hands scratching at the uphill slope for balance, his progress was so painfully slow that the poor man's afternoon out would have amounted to no more than a kilometre each way. Farther from safety and in deteriorating weather, his predicament could have become serious and the moral is clear.

Experienced mountain walkers need no lessons in equipping themselves appropriately, but those less sure might benefit from the notes which follow. Although it is perfectly possible to enjoy some of the routes dressed in casual attire, particularly in fine settled weather, most of the walks in this guidebook demand a robust and carefully considered range of gear. In certain conditions, that gear will be crucially important – even lifesaving.

**Footwear**
On the lower paths, stout shoes with a good tread will suffice, but on intermediate and higher trails, boots which keep stones and snow out and support the ankles are essential. The earlier in the year your visit takes place, the more snow and ice you will encounter. Boots with some mid-sole rigidity provide a firmer platform on which to 'bite' into paths over snow than very flexible ones. Making sure the boots

are waxed (if leather!) will help prevent wet feet when crossing snowfields or streams, as will the wearing of gaiters or elasticated anklets. Articulated plastic boots are gaining in popularity, but seem a little clumsy on lower stretches of trail where their impermeability and rigidity are redundant. Whatever you wear, try to establish a good level of foot comfort before embarking on long walks, since alpine gradients and terrain are sure to reveal any insipient problems!

**Clothing**
The pleasures of summer walking are often enhanced by wearing a lightweight shirt and shorts. Indeed, given a modicum of fine weather, limbs may well get suntanned on your visit to Chamonix-Mont-Blanc: equally, of course, they may not! When the sun shines, valley temperatures soar, but at altitude its warming effect may be nullified by lower air temperatures, wind chill and the cooling influence of surrounding snow. So moving up from warm valley to high trail calls for versatile clothing.

The key to comfort is avoiding excess body heat or chill and this is achieved more readily by employing several thin layers of clothing than by relying on one heavy anorak or sweater. In sunny conditions, shorts are still adequate if combined with a polar jacket or a couple of thin sweaters over a shirt; many, however, will prefer to wear breeches.

Zip, button or velcro front fastenings allow air to circulate round the torso when climbing; uncovering pulse points at wrist and neck will also help you keep cool. With a little thought, it is possible to 'fine tune' ventilation and remain comfortable at all levels of activity.

Summer sunlight in the Alps is very strong, whatever the ambient air temperature. A brimmed or peaked sunhat will protect your head from overheating and will help shade the eyes. A lightweight woolly hat and even gloves might be appreciated if you are camping high or overnighting in high refuges and making early starts.

With less threat from biting cold and wind-driven rain than British hill-walkers are accustomed to, many continentals use waterproof capes instead of cagoule and overtrousers. The latter however are more versatile – if 'breathable' they can be used as windproofs and are infinitely preferable in a survival or rescue situation. Weather can change suddenly and dramatically in the Alps so good shell clothing should always be carried. (See 'Mountain Safety')

**Equipment**

Since the majority of walks in this guidebook can be accomplished in a day, it will be assumed that backpackers who wish to link up routes into longer itineraries or to camp high as an accommodation option will simply add their gear to day-walk requirements.

A rucsac is a necessity, one with the capacity to hold spare clothing, food, miscellaneous items, and with loops to carry an ice-axe. Inside the rucsac can be kept a small first-aid kit (eg. plasters, triangular bandage, antiseptic cream, painkillers, safety pins, string, emergency whistle, telephone coins, etc.). Other essential items include polarising sunglasses or snow-goggles, sunblock or glacier cream, emergency energy rations and small torch, liquid and food on routes with no refreshment points, shell clothing and gaiters or anklets. A map case is useful for holding map, compass and guidebook in wet weather, as are plastic liners to keep rucsac contents dry. If a camera is carried, film is best packed deep in the rucsac to remain cool.

On many sections of trail above about 2000m (6500ft), lying snow (névé) will be encountered and an ice-axe is useful – normally to aid balance as a 'third leg', but occasionally to safeguard against a fall on steep snowslopes. A practical alternative for most situations is a steel-tipped walking stick or staff.

Finally, if it is planned to stay overnight in refuges, a sheet sleeping bag and indoor shoes (trainers or moccasins) should be carried.

# MAPS

Sketch-maps accompanying the text of this guidebook are drawn to scale and contain sufficient information to enable walkers to identify major features and keep a check on progress during a walk. However, there are good reasons for carrying map and compass as well. If the trail is lost in mist or in error, a map becomes an essential navigational aid; should deteriorating weather, injury, illness or accident dictate choosing an alternative routing – perhaps an immediate retreat to the valley – map and compass provide a key to the problem; and distant features in the landscape can be accurately pin-pointed, thus increasing your appreciation and knowledge of the region.

I.G.N. (Institut Géographique National), the French equivalent to the British Ordnance Survey, produce three excellent sheets which together embrace the area of this guidebook. Detail is carefully drawn, long-distance trails are marked and prominent footpaths overprinted in red. The sheets are in the blue 'Carte Topographique' series, scale 1:25,000, numbers 3630 West (Chamonix-Mont-Blanc, including Vallorcine and Argentière); 3530 East (Passy and the Desert de Platé); 3531 East (St. Gervais-les-Bains, including the Contamines-Montjoie valley).

Maps and guides can be purchased or ordered from your local book or outdoor shop. They can usually be bought from stock at Stanfords Ltd., 12-14 Long Acre, Covent Garden, London WC2E 9LP; at McCarta Ltd. 122 Kings Cross Road, London WC1X 9DS and at YHA Bookshop, 14 Southampton Street, Covent Garden, London WC2E 7HY. French bookshops and newsagents sell them too! Guidebooks to the Tour du Mont Blanc and GR5 Traverse of the Alps, mentioned in the text, are published by Cicerone Press and these too are available at Stanfords, McCarta and the YHA Bookshop.

In the USA, maps can be obtained from Rand McNally Map Store, 10 E. 53rd St., New York or Pacific Travellers, 529 State St., Santa Barbara CA93101.

Additional information on walking, accommodation, entertainments, sporting facilities etc. around Chamonix-Mont-Blanc is available from local information centres and from the French Government Tourist Office, 178 Piccadilly, London W1. or 610 5th Ave., New York, NY 10020.

# MOUNTAIN SAFETY

There is an element of risk in alpine walking which even the best prepared are not immune to. Stonefall, path subsidence, losing the way in mist, a slip on wet rock or ice, disabling injury or illness and exposure to the weather all belong to a category of unpredictable experience which threatens our equilibrium. Often the threat is slight, a mere inconvenience, but occasionally events occur in which our very survival may be at stake. Alternatively, you might be witness to someone else's misfortune and be called upon to act.

If there is a refuge or chalet within reasonable walking distance, help can be summoned by telephoning **Chamonix Mountain Rescue** on **(50) 53.16.89.** Ensure the victim is safe, warm, comfortable and preferably still accompanied before leaving him/her.

If no telephone is near at hand, the international distress call should be employed. This consists of 6 visual or audial signals per minute, followed by a minute's pause and then repeated. The reply is 3 such signals per minute, with a minute's pause before repeating.

*Rescue helicopter above the Desert de Platé*

Distress signals are made in the most appropriate way, depending on conditions and available material, eg. blowing a whistle, shouting, flashing a torch in darkness or a mirror in sunshine, etc.

Another generally recognised signal, particularly from the air, is to raise both arms straight up to indicate 'I need help'. Raising one arm only means you do not require assistance. Helicopter rescue is fairly commonplace in the Chamonix-Mont-Blanc region, but unless insurance has been taken out covering such an eventuality, you will be left holding a sizeable bill (check the small print of your policy). Much depends on the severity of the situation and money may well not be a prime consideration.

Risks can be minimised by ensuring that you and your gear are in a fit condition for planned itineraries, that items of emergency equipment and energy rations are carried, and that if possible someone knows your route and expected time of return.

# WEATHER, AND OBTAINING A FORECAST

Being aware of unfolding weather patterns and conversant with the signs which precede change are vital elements in mountain safety. As you might expect, weather around Mont Blanc is different in many respects to that generally experienced over British hills and the following notes, whilst not written by a meteorologist, sketch in an outline of summer conditions in the region.

In fact, the Mont Blanc massif forms a line of demarcation between Atlantic, Continental and Mediterranean weather types, also generating a number of micro-climates of its own: while Mont Blanc itself and peaks to the north-east are gripped by violent storms, the Chamonix valley and Aiguilles Rouges may be enjoying fine weather for example.

In general terms, Haute-Savoie is characterised by a moist, cool and temperate climate. Abundant water from melting snow during the summer months sustains luxuriant vegetation, but permanent human settlement is possible only at relatively low altitudes and in sheltered valleys. Typical summer temperatures at Chamonix range from 17 to 23 deg. C, with rainfall heaviest (130mm) in July.

Although periods of disturbed weather do occur during the summer, there is a tendency towards weak atmospheric circulation with low wind speeds – a situation somewhat removed from the often volatile hill weather of Britain. In this part of the Alps, vertical air movement due to thermal exchanges is more pronounced than horizontal movement of whole air masses, though exceptions will always prove the rule!

Disturbed summer weather takes three main forms. First a daily weather cycle unfolding over consecutive 24 hour periods, during which a still, clear morning is succeeded by building cumulus. From midday onwards these large clouds obscure ground above 2000m, towering above the higher massifs and culminating in thunderstorms. The thermal effect of the sun's radiation on unstable air in the lower atmosphere is responsible, so the cooler evenings are often fine and clear.

The second form is the approximate 10-day cycle. In improving weather, winds are mainly from the northern sector, air temperatures are low, visibility excellent. Within two or three days fine conditions seem well established, but with each succeeding 24 hours the air temperature rises until, approaching the 8th or 9th day, high level winds strengthen from the south-west and the sky clouds up rapidly with heavy cumulo-nimbus producing thunderstorms. Movement on mountain trails can be impossible for several hours under the onslaught of squally winds, torrential downpours, low cloud base and sudden drops in temperature.

If a thunderstorm is imminent, try to avoid these places: summits and ridges; cliff edges or high cairns; vertical clefts and caves, including stream beds; beneath isolated trees; lake shores; close to metal objects. If caught out in the open, aim for trees lower than the average tree height of the surrounding area, or below and between flat boulders, or kneel with hands on knees, head well down, preferably on an insulating layer or rucsac etc. Easier said than done, but a lightning strike will earth via your arms and knees rather than your head and heart! Better still, keep a weather eye open and make intelligent route decisions.

The third form of summer bad weather is the slow-moving front. Less commonly encountered than previous categories, this one is characterised by a cloudy sky, often with a ceiling at around 4000m. Rain falls spasmodically but winds are feeble, even at high altitude. For walkers and climbers it is a wet, depressing time, unlikely to inspire a challenging route or a memorable day on the trail. Such conditions change only slowly and may persist for many days.

Cloud formations over Mont Blanc can provide important clues for weather prediction. The more unequivocal sky signs are generally acknowledged to be reliable indicators and have become part of local folk-lore. For example, if Mont Blanc 'smokes his pipe', strong winds are blowing at altitude – clouds streaming from the high ridges are spindrift. If Mont Blanc 'wears a bonnet', a storm is promised – summits are buried in a mass of heavy cloud. Double lens-shaped clouds trailing to the east of Mont Blanc – 'l'Ane' – is a frequent precursor of rain and cloud. A 'Foehn' wind, scouring the high valleys and glaciers to the south of the region often leaves the north with sunny periods and pleasantly warm temperatures.

Amounts of sunshine received throughout the year may well determine a mountainside's entire micro-climate. Whether it faces north or south can have far-reaching effects on flora and fauna since lying snow will linger in shady locations, sometimes failing to melt at all. A less predictable factor is the march of weather patterns producing in some years light snowfall and an early spring, in others a relentless winter whose bitter after-taste can be sensed well into August.

**Obtaining a Weather Forecast**
Detailed weather bulletins are posted each morning at Tourist

Information Offices throughout the region and at other town centre locations in Chamonix. This information is updated at the main Tourist Offices once, and sometimes twice, during the day. Data is comprehensive (but in French!) although the Meteorological Service freely acknowledge the problems of prediction in such a topographically complex and varied area. In the author's experience these bulletins can usually be relied upon, tending if anything towards the pessimistic rather than the optimistic. Tourist Office staff will do their best to help translate into English if required.

Pre-recorded weather forecasts (again in French) are available by ringing (50)53.03.40. Weather maps ('Meteo') appear in both regional and national newspapers. Terminology is fairly constant, so if your French is shaky a dictionary will soon unravel the linguistic mysteries! A further valuable source of weather information are the guardians of refuges whose familiarity with the mountain scene qualifies them to give an informed opinion.

# NATURE RESERVES, FLORA AND FAUNA

Conservation is a pressing issue in the Mont Blanc region, for not only do eco-systems groan beneath the seasonal onslaught of visitors' feet and skis, but for some reason our continental friends and fellow walkers are inclined rather to take their alpine environment for granted! The author, in company no doubt with many readers, has witnessed the indiscriminate picking of wild flowers, both in Britain and abroad. Nothing in his experience, however, surpasses for blatant ecological vandalism the sight of a family near Plaine Joux armed with trowels and wooden crates excavating whole banks of alpine plants to carry home for the vase or garden!

With increasing public awareness high on a list of priorities, three Nature Reserves have been set up in the area covered by this guidebook. The Aiguilles Rouges Reserve, created in 1974, is well represented at the Col des Montets Interpretation Centre and Laboratory north of Argentière. There are audio-visual displays, charts, pictures, books for sale and an informatively laid out 'ecological trail' on adjacent hillside. The conservation message is clear and there is detailed information on mountain flora and fauna.

Instigated in 1980, the Passy Nature Reserve concerns itself primarily with explaining the geology of Mont Blanc and its environs. This is appropriate, since just to the north of the Information Centre at Plaine-Joux, above Plateau d'Assy, rises a great limestone upland of unique interest.

*In the pastoral Contamines-Montjoie valley*

Lakes, torrents, snow and glaciers are the domain of the Contamines-Montjoie Nature Reserve, inaugurated in 1979, though at the time of writing there is no permanent exhibition or visitor centre.

Vegetation grows profusely on the lower and intermediate slopes around Mont Blanc, changing in size and type as altitude is gained. From valley to tree-line, many plants and flowers common to Britain and the Alps thrive, along with exclusively native species. Travelling upwards, you pass through luxuriant meadows and shady forest of pine and larch and are likely to come across the magnificent spires of the Yellow Gentian. Also to be found among numerous other species are Martagon lilies and some of the many diverse orchids.

Plants such as juniper, birch and alder grow stunted and sparse at the upper tree-line, eventually giving way to true alpine plants. Dwarf Alpenrose with its pink bell-shaped flowers thrives up to 2800m (9000ft). Other high-pasture flowers include the gaily coloured purple and yellow Alpine Aster and the large blue Trumpet Gentian.

Higher still, thin grass gives way to rock and scree, but even here flowers grow in clefts and cracks. Among these jewels of high mountain places are Rock Jasmine, the delicate purple heads of the Alpine Pansy and the bright blue Spring Gentian.

Birds, mammals and insects are as diverse as the flora, but many are endangered by man's spreading occupation of the land. Specific hill species such as marmot and mountain hare are sometimes encountered on the high trails, but less commonly here than in other parts of Haute-Savoie. Chamois were once in evidence, but alas have retreated to less accessible pockets of mountainside to the west of Mont Blanc. Needless to say, the brown bear of the Vallorcine forests has long since disappeared!

It is some consolation that while walkers and climbers enjoy the Mont Blanc area's quite exceptional scenery and amenities, to the undoubted detriment of indiginous wildlife, other less popular areas in this sector of the Alps still provide refuge for thriving populations of mountain-dwelling creatures.

# TOPOGRAPHY AND GLACIERS

To delve into the geological complexities of how the Alps were formed lies outside the scope of this book. However, it is possible to draw a broad outline of the Mont Blanc area's salient features and their origins.

Some 770 million years ago, an upheaval of the earth's crust raised a mass of schists, gneiss and limestone to form the underlying axis of the Alps range. Towards the end of this upheaval, around 300 million years ago, intrusions of granite in the western sector of these ancient mountains brought with them metamorphic rocks which together formed the base of what we now know as the Mont Blanc and Aiguilles Rouges massifs.

Following extensive erosion and inundation by the sea when beds of sedimentary rock were laid down, this part of the Alps underwent a new phase of elevation as violent movements in the continental 'plates' produced great mountain-building creasings of the earth's crust. The formation of Mont Blanc was completed towards the end of this Tertiary Era, some 15 millions years ago. These complex and cataclysmic movements were succeeded in the Quartenary Era by the formation of huge glaciers whose action helped to sculpt the present profile of the Mont Blanc range and excavated the Chamonix valley, at that time buried beneath 1000m of ice.

Under the influence of a warming climate, the glaciers have

retreated but still play a major role in erosion. Other eroding agencies whose evidence is clear to see are the freeze-thaw cycles of moisture in the form of ice, frost and snow which can split and flake rock; meltwater and rain scouring channels down mountainsides and carrying with it boulders, stones and sediment; wind which displaces already loose material; avalanche and landslip flattening downslope vegetation and changing land drainage patterns; and man whose feet, wheels, activities and constructions play their part in modifying the environment.

There are five connected but distinct areas covered by the walks in this guidebook. The main Chamonix/River Arve valley, sandwiched between the Aiguilles Rouges and Mont Blanc massifs, lies at the heart of this region with the Vallorcine, Argentière, Servoz and Contamines-Montjoie valley areas forming extensions at either end.

*Vallorcine*: Beyond Col des Montets, a less-frequented 'pocket' of spectacular mountains and valleys unfolds. It is bounded by the Swiss frontier and Émosson lakes to the north, Aiguillette des Posettes to the east, and provides access to the Aiguilles Rouges massif in the west via the Bérard and Tré-les-Eaux valleys. Deeply afforested and rich in alpine flora, it is an area with few 'tourist attractions' other than a couple of excellent refuges. Walks range from strenuous to easy.

*Argentière*: Technically within the Chamonix valley, this area takes in the headwaters of the River Arve and Col de Balme on the Swiss frontier. To the east, two major glaciers are visited – Le Tour and Argentière – close to a number of imposing peaks, among them Aiguille du Chardonnet and Aiguille Verte. From Argentière and old Le Tour village, mechanical lifts run up mountainsides popular with winter skiiers and summer walkers alike. Two longer-distance trails running the entire length of the Chamonix valley start at Argentière.

*Chamonix*: Tourist hub of the Mont Blanc region. The busy valley is held between the Brévent and Aiguilles Rouges to the north-west, Mont Blanc to the south-east and high ground to the west of Les Houches. Walks at various levels explore north and south facing valley sides, including the Mer de Glace, Bossons, Tacconnaz and Bionnassay glaciers. Many other dramatic features are encompassed – rock peaks, lakes, waterfalls, cols, ridges and summits, while several cable-cars, cabin-lifts and two rack-and-pinion railways reach

*On Montagne de la Côte above Taconnaz Glacier*

to around 2000m altitude. Mid-height 'balcon' trails offer classic views of the Chamonix Aiguilles and Mont Blanc.

*Servoz*: At the west end of the Chamonix valley, the Diosaz and Souay torrents join the River Arve at Servoz. Near their sources lies Col d'Anterne, a notch in a long line of vertical cliffs bordering a unique and sensational limestone upland. Lower slopes around Plateau d'Assy are renowned for their health-restoring sanatoria and winter skiing. Rock scenery is extraordinary, the walks exciting and summer visitors thinner on the ground.

*The Contamines-Montjoie valley*: Separated from Chamonix by a long spur thrown down north-west from Aiguille de Bionnassay, this area has a character all its own. The Bon Nant river flows due north to enter the Arve near St. Gervais-les-Bains, the largest resort. Beneath precipitous Mont Joly, however, the delightful small town of Les Contamines-Montjoie is the area's fulcrum. Lofty ridges enclose the valley head at Col du Bonhomme and walks extend even further to summit and ridge. Lakes, cols, high alps and refuges act as focal points for walks.

**Glaciers**

Seven major glaciers and several minor ones are encountered on walks described in this guidebook. For many visitors these vast white tongues of frozen water (Mer de Glace alone is estimated to contain approximately 4 thousand million cubic metres) epitomise the alpine scene. There is nothing like them in British mountains, in lower European ranges or in massifs farther south, and their dazzling presence stamps itself indelibly onto the senses.

Climbing to glacier moraines and points adjacent to their higher reaches, as some walks do, is an enthralling experience and represents the closest that mountain walkers come to the domain of the fully initiated mountaineer. Because of the intrinsic fascination attached to glaciers, the following notes have been added to help readers understand and appreciate the natural forces which spawn and shape them.

Water in its solid state is extremely hard and brittle, light enough to float in liquid water and capable of flowing like a river under pressure. Glaciers form where more snow falls in winter than melts away in summer. Settled snow undergoes structural changes which increase its density and this compaction results in a completely bonded zone of rigid ice. This layer is subject to fracturing and

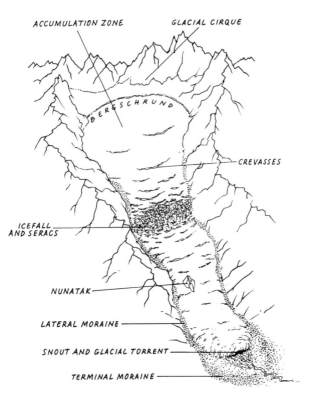

*Diagrammatic profile of a valley glacier*

cracking, forming crevasses as the glacial mass slowly slips downhill. Immense internal pressure raises the ice's melting point and the resultant meltwater acts as a lubricant, but most glacial movement is due to the ice's own plasticity. Ice crystals deformed by the huge weight above then slide over each other, much as discs of shiny plastic would.

Valley glaciers in the Mont Blanc area form above the permanent snow line and become elongated channels of ice terminating in a snout well below the snow line. That they 'flow' was noticed by accident when articles – even human bodies – lost high on glaciers reappeared decades later downstream. A line of posts set straight

*Practising ice climbing techniques on the Bossons Glacier*

across a glacier will point downhill in a U-shaped arc after some months have elapsed. Longitudinal stripes and V-shaped chevrons of rock debris on a glacier's surface relate to summer rockfalls and erosion cycles; winter rockfalls are less frequent and become snow covered.

Rates of flow vary, as do patterns of advance and retreat. Around 1700, during a period of severe winters, the Mer de Glace threatened to obstruct the Arve valley and local inhabitants resorted to 'exorcism' of the evil glacier spirits in the hope of halting the great wall of ice. In 1825, Les Bois village was evacuated, but since the turn of the century this and other glaciers fringing Mont Blanc have significantly receded.

Crevasses, or tension cracks, occur where the glacier passes over irregularities in the valley floor and are mostly crescent-shaped. Where they intersect, 'seracs' are formed (ice pinnacles). Sometimes the underlying ground is so rough and steep that seracs and ice-cliffs tumble on the verge of avalanche, a dangerous zone for humans to penetrate. Occasional minor rock peaks high enough to protrude through the glacier surface appear as dark islands and are technically known as 'nunataks', an Eskimo term. In the French Alps they are often referred to as 'rognons'.

Glacial torrents – the River Arve is a good example – are milky green in colour from a heavy suspension of finely ground rock dust. Glaciers are great movers of earth and rocks, straightening out valleys, sawing off intruding spurs and ridges, polishing and trimming the land in their ponderous response to gravity's pull. Higher still, the glacier's birthplace will be marked by a 'cirque' ('cwm' in Wales, 'corrie' in Scotland) and a 'bergschrund' or 'rimaye' – a gap where freeze-thaw cycles have pulled the ice away from the mountain headwall. Cirques which are progressively etched away by glacial ice steepen, and by submitting to similar erosion from other directions can form knife-edge ridges and tooth-shaped peaks.

Specific skills and hardware should be acquired before venturing onto a glacier's surface. Snow conceals crevasses and ice is a difficult medium to negotiate.

*Notre-Dame-de-la-Gorge*

# FEATURES ENCOUNTERED ON THE WALKS

Walk                          **GLACIERS**
3   The Tré-les-Eaux Valley.
7   The Albert Premier Refuge.
9   The Argentière Glacier.
15  Montenvers to Plan de l'Aiguille: the Grand Balcon Nord.
18  Gare des Glaciers.
19  Montagne de la Côte and La Jonction.
21  Col de Voza, Mont-Lachat and Le Nid d'Aigle.
26  Col de Tricot.


**SUMMITS**
2   Aiguillette des Posettes and Col des Montets.
8   Tête du Grand Chantet.
11  Montroc to Les Houches: Grand Balcon Sud and Le Brévent.
20  Lac du Brévent and Aiguillette des Houches.
22  Le Prarion from Les Houches.
25  Le Prarion from Bionnay.
27  Mont Joly.
31  Col du Bonhomme and La Croix-du-Bonhomme Refuge.


**COLS**
2   Aiguillette des Posettes and Col des Montets.
4   The Pierre à Bérard Refuge and Col de Salenton.
5   Tour of the Aiguilles Rouges.
6   Col de Balme and Source of the River Arve.
11  Montroc to Les Houches: Grand Balcon Sud and Le Brévent.
16  The Cornu and Noirs Lakes.
21  Col de Voza, Mont-Lachat and Le Nid d'Aigle.
22  Le Prarion from Les Houches.
23  Col d'Anterne.
25  Le Prarion from Bionnay.
26  Col de Tricot.
29  Col de la Fenêtre.
31  Col du Bonhomme and La Croix-du-Bonhomme Refuge.


**LAKES**
1   The Loriaz Refuge and Émosson Lakes.
13  La Flégère and Lac Blanc.

14 L'Índex, Lac Blanc and the Chéserys Lakes.
16 The Cornu and Noirs Lakes.
20 Lac du Brévent and Aiguillette des Houches.
23 Col d'Anterne.
28 The Tré-la-Tête Refuge and Lac d'Armancette.
30 The Jovet Lakes.

**REFUGES**
1   The Loriaz Refuge and Émosson Lakes.
4   The Pierre à Bérard Refuge and Col de Salenton.
5   Tour of the Aiguilles Rouges.
6   Col de Balme and source of the River Arve.
7   The Albert Premier Refuge.
11  Montroc to Les Houches: Grand Balcon Sud and Le Brévent.
13  La Flégère and Lac Blanc.
14  L'Index, Lac Blanc and the Chéserys Lakes.
15  Montenvers to Plan de l'Aiguille: The Grand Balcon Nord.
19  Montagne de la Côte and La Jonction.
20  Lac du Brévent and Aiguillette des Houches.
21  Col de Voza, Mont-Lachat and Le Nid d'Aigle.
22  Le Prarion from Les Houches.
23  Col d'Anterne.
24  Desert de Platé and the Platé Refuge.
25  Le Prarion from Bionnay.
26  Col de Tricot.
27  Mont Joly.
28  The Tré-la-Tête Refuge and Lac d'Armancette.
29  Col de la Fenêtre.
30  The Jovet Lakes.
31  Col du Bonhomme and La Croix-du-Bonhomme Refuge.

**VALLEYS**
3   The Tré-les-Eaux Valley.
4   The Pierre à Bérard Refuge and Col de Salenton.
10  Argentière to Servoz: The Petit Balcon Sud.

**'BALCON' PATHS**
10  Argentière to Servoz: The Petit Balcon Sud.
11  Montroc to Les Houches: Grand Balcon Sud and Le Brévent.
12  Chalets de la Pendant and the Petit Balcon Nord.
15  Montenvers to Plan de l'Aiguille: The Grand Balcon Nord.

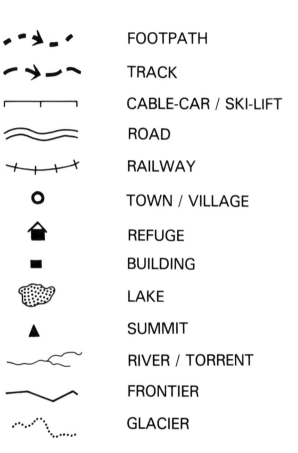

FOOTPATH

TRACK

CABLE-CAR / SKI-LIFT

ROAD

RAILWAY

TOWN / VILLAGE

REFUGE

BUILDING

LAKE

SUMMIT

RIVER / TORRENT

FRONTIER

GLACIER

# 1:
# The Vallorcine Area

*Les Grands Montets (top) from Les Granges*

## Walk 1    The Loriaz Refuge and Émosson Lakes

Routing:  Vallorcine – Le Crot – Loriaz Refuge – Montagne de
            Barberine – Lac d'Émosson – Barberine forest – Vallor-
            cine.
Total ascent: 815m (2674ft).
Timings:  Ascent to Loriaz Refuge – 2 hours.
            Loriaz Refuge to Lac d'Émosson – 1½ hours.
            Descent to Vallorcine – 2 hours.

Meals, snacks, drinks and accommodation available at the Loriaz
Refuge.
*Special note: There are some exposed scrambly stretches on the
'balcon' traverse equipped with metal holds in places, and in very early
season (eg. before July) an ice-axe might be needed to safeguard the
crossing of steep snowbanks.*

Although close to the Swiss frontier (the Émosson lakes are actually
in Switzerland) and therefore some distance topographically from
Mont Blanc, fascinating views of the massif are gained from the
middle section of this walk. It is an expedition full of surprises, from
the quiet, unfrequented climb and a welcoming hut to an increasingly
rugged finale along and below Montagne de Barberine, taking in
spectacular lakes and two fine waterfalls on the descent. The route
provides walkers with an excellent appreciation of this less-visited,
north-eastern corner of the Chamonix area; it is an equally fine
itinerary in the reverse direction.

Situated on the N506 road north of Col des Montets, **Vallorcine** is a
smaller place than a glance at the map would suggest, its importance
as a frontier railway station taking precedence over amenities. There
are, however, a few hotels, bars and restaurants, a small general
store and a Gîte d'étape with camping. There is also a generous car
park by the S.N.C.F. station and a Syndicat d'Initiative (Tourist
Information) kiosk which displays an up-to-date weather forecast.
Starting here, walk up to the main road and turn right. In about
250m, turn left past the Gîte d'étape campsite, and left again up a
lane signed 'Le Crot and Refuge de Loriaz'. Go between the chalets,
turning left then right through their backyards! (the way is
indicated.) The thin path passes through long-abandoned cultivation
terraces and climbs gently in lush grasses and beautiful flora, veering
north-west. Already there are good views back to Mont Blanc.

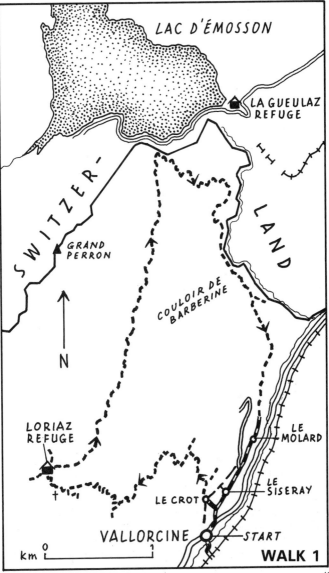

LAC D'ÉMOSSON

LA GUEULAZ
REFUGE

SWITZER-

LAND

GRAND
PERRON

COULOIR DE
BARBERINE

N

LORIAZ
REFUGE

LE
MOLARD

LE CROT

LE
SISERAY

VALLORCINE

START

km 0                    1

**WALK 1**

As you rise towards a line of grey cliffs, keep left (south-west). Gaining height steadily in zig-zags, the path becomes better defined, though the trees on this south-facing hillside so far have been too small to provide any shade should it be sought. The next line of cliffs under Tête du Taltet are also passed to the left, whereafter the path winds in and out round rocky bluffs and enters mature pine forest.

Pass a junction down left to La Nant and continue on the zig-zags, soon out above the treeline, past banks of dwarf alpenrose. A boulder waymark announces the proximity of the refuge as an exceptionally wide panorama begins to unfold. Dominating to the north-west is Pointe de la Terrasse (2734m – 8970ft) and its col, which can be attained from the refuge but by a more difficult grade of route than this guidebook contains, especially when there is still considerable snow cover.

Nearing a large cross, the path from Le Couteray joins in from the left for the final 500m to the **Loriaz Refuge** (2020m – 6627ft. Renovated recently by the Vallorcine Commune; 30 places; guardian during the summer months, closed in winter. Meals, snacks and drinks, including a superb spring of clear, ice-cold drinking water issuing from a pipe!) There is a distinctly farm-like flavour to the hut, with its rows of neat, restored outbuildings and its setting on a broad shelf of upland pasture.

You walk between the refuge and outbuildings, past a 'rustic' WC and the path off left to Col de la Terrasse (2648m – 8687ft). Now begins an exhilarating 'balcon' traverse at mid-height between the heavily forested valley and the high frontier ridge culminating in the Grand Perron (2673m – 8770ft). As well as gazing across to the Argentière massif (Aiguille Verte, the Drus, etc.) and Col de Balme at the northern end of the Chamonix valley, keep a good eye open for Mont Blanc and the Chamonix Aiguilles, seen to great advantage from this angle.

As the path undulates gently along, over possible snowbanks in gullies, the vegetated slopes seem to fall away almost vertically to Vallorcine 770m (2550ft) below. A boulder field is crossed and the way starts to climb beneath an electricity pylon and up rough mountainside. Presumably, many of the orange paint flashes hereabouts would be obscured by snow early in the summer, hence their profusion!

In the middle of this traverse is a vertiginous drop into the **Couloir de Barberine** and if the path here should be snow covered, extreme caution is required for reasons which need no further elaboration! Just how formidable this cleft is in the architecture of Montagne de

*Aiguille de Loriaz from Refuge de Loriaz*

Barberine will be seen as our descent passes its base.

More rocky passages are negotiated above big drops, but in the more exposed places metal holds have been fixed for additional security and the path is quite safe with care. Rocky corners and boulders follow each other in tortuous succession – a much more strenuous section, this – until suddenly the great crescent-shaped dam of **Lac d'Émosson** is in view ahead below Bel Oiseau peak.

Unbelievably, a mountain railway runs across the precipice opposite, a small red train which squeaks gingerly along – the Chemin de Fer d'Émosson. It connects with the Funiculaire de

*Distant Mont Blanc and the Chamonix Aiguilles
from Montagne de Barberine*

Barberine from Le Châtelard in the valley just inside Switzerland. From the top end of the railway, a lift takes passengers up to La Grueulaz Refuge-Cabane and the dam itself, with a viewing table.

Climbing over a final rocky spur, down slabs and over more boulders, you reach **Col du Passet** (1950 – 6398ft), right on the Swiss border. To the left (west) is a viewpoint worth detouring to, for as well as revealing more of the vast Lac d'Émosson, there is a dramatic glimpse of the smaller Lac du Vieux Émosson, often dotted with ice-floes and cradled within a forbidding amphitheatre of cliffs. For a closer look at the joint Franco-Swiss dam, a path drops to the access road 100m away.

A large waymarked rock at Col du Passet indicates the route down right to Vallorcine. At first it descends quite abruptly by the side of a small stream on loose slopes strewn with stones. Passing a small waterfall, you cross a rocky stream bed and rapidly lose height in a long series of twists and turns through patchy forest. At some slabs and a waymark post, Vallorcine is signed right, 50min., but 1½ hours is more realistic.

Quite unexpectedly, the path now leads out round the head of a wild combe in which rugged, bouldery slopes rise to the soaring vertical buttresses of Montagne de Barberine. At the base of these cliffs, the path descends over rocky steps and, lower down, passes an impressive waterfall in a narrow ravine – the **Grand Cascade de Barberine**. It flows out into an idyllic, crystal-clear pool, but signs warn of the dangers from sudden changes in water level due to hydro-electric flow controls. Armed with first-hand knowledge that this benign little stream flows directly from the Émosson dam above, only walkers with a chronic deficit of imagination will submit to the temptation to take a dip!

That the surrounding slopes are prime avalanche country can be in no doubt – witness the broken tree trunks, shattered rocks and other debris all around the path. The Couloir de Barberine (whose top was crossed earlier) from here is a long, almost vertical stone chute penetrating sinister rock walls.

Soon after dropping into forest, a path leaves left to the Cascade du Dard (about 300m away) and we fork right to Valorcine. The route contours round still-chaotic slopes of stones and fallen trees, but the forest ambience is much more pleasant. Joined by a path from the left (to Barberine hamlet), we pass a ruined chalet then an intact one and cross the Nant du Rand on a plank bridge, now directly above the N506 road and the noisy Eau Noire torrent.

Still thoroughly delightful, the path emerges from forest and leads past chalets onto the tarred road at **Le Mollard**. Follow it along past Le Clos church, through Le Siceray hamlet to the Gîte d'étape campsite and the road at Vallorcine. Walk up the road and turn left to the station car park.

### Walk 2   Aiguillette des Posettes and Col des Montets
Routing: Vallorcine – Les Saix Blanc – Col des Posettes – Aiguillette des Posettes – Tête du Chenavier – Col des Montets – Le Buet – Vallorcine.
Total ascent: 941m (3087ft).

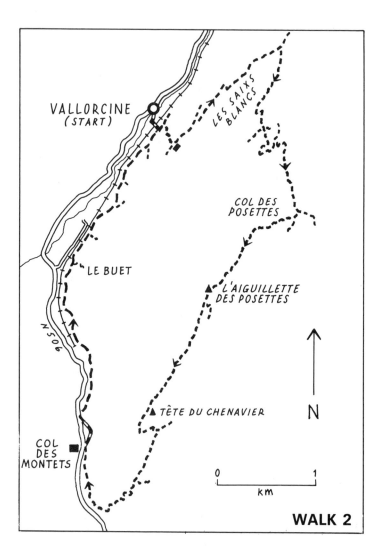

VALLORCINE
(START)

LES SAIXS BLANCS

COL DES
POSETTES

LE BUET

N 506

▲ L'AIGUILLETTE
DES POSETTES

▲ TÊTE DU CHENAVIER

COL
DES
MONTETS

N

0                    1
km

**WALK 2**

Timings: Vallorcine to Aiguillette des Posettes – 3 hours.
   Aiguillette des Posettes to Col des Montets – 1¼ hours.
   Col des Montets to Vallorcine – 1¼ hours.

Drinks and snacks available at the buvette in the Aiguilles Rouges Nature Reserve Interpretation Centre on Col des Montets.
*Special note: Early in the summer, snow may still be lying on the summit ridge of Aiguillette des Posettes when care is needed.*

The heavy mantle of spruce trees which clothe the hillside above Vallorcine feed neighbouring sawmills, while the higher pastures constitute one of the last locations in the Chamonix area on which cattle are grazed, the onslaught of tourism having largely squeezed out traditional husbandry.

From above Col des Posettes, the walk takes to the ridge separating the Arve headwaters and the villages of Le Tour and Montroc from the valley of the Eau Noire, which carries main road and railway through Vallorcine and into Switzerland. This ridge holds the narrow, rocky summit of Aiguillette des Posettes but broadens out on its descent to Col des Montets.

Here is found the principal interface between the general public (motorists and walkers alike) and the Aiguilles Rouges Nature Reserve, a popular stopping-off point for visitors to the region. Thereafter, the walk never strays far from the N506 road and the railway but remains on paths and tracks for the descent to Vallorcine.

**Vallorcine**, on the N506 north of Col des Montets, contains a small food store, a buffet/bar at the S.N.C.F. railway station, several hotels, a Gîte d'étape with camping and a Tourist Information kiosk adjacent to the large station car park where the walk begins.

Walk to the right (south) of the station buildings, cross the railway line and turn left in front of the Hôtel des Voyageurs (bar/créperie). In about 25m, go over a stile right, signed 'Les Posettes', and climb on a path over grassy hillside to the Part du Plan Chalets. Here the route swings left (north-east – in fact, a now little-used variant of the Tour du Mont Blanc, hence the red and white waymarks in places.)

In a few hundred metres, ignore a path off left and continue climbing through conifer trees in Bois de la Planche. At the first zig-zag, keep to the main path which rises to meet a good track at **Les Saix Blancs** (1700m – 5577ft). Here turn right. The track winds its way on up past the odd clearing and as it begins to emerge onto more open ground, a junction is passed down right, leading back to Le Buet in the valley.

49

Continue up the side of a small combe, short-cut a big bend and come out onto grassy mountainside below avalanche fences, keeping in a south-east direction to arrive at **Col des Posettes** (1997m – 6552ft). Ahead, the Arve valley drops gently away and a wide panorama unfolds, a panorama still to be enlarged and sharpened during the next leg of the walk.

Follow the path south-west towards Ardoissières for about 100m, then branch off right uphill towards the ridge line which leads to the summit of **l'Aiguillette des Posettes** at 2201m (7221ft). This rocky viewpoint, joined from the north-west by another craggy ridge, is particularly fine owing to its isolated position. The Chamonix Aiguilles, pointed spires of varying height and shape from the Aiguille des Grands Montets to the Aiguille du Midi, pierce the south-western skyline and lead on to the snowy dome of Mont Blanc. To the north-east lies Col de Balme, a dip in the frontier ridge with Switzerland, while to the west stands Mont Buet and Val de Tré-les-Eaux (see Walk 3).

Stay along the ridge top (south-west) which rapidly grows wider and crosses just to the right of a lower eminence – Tête du Chenavier (1927m – 6322ft), from where there is an excellent view down to Vallorcine and our return route. Shortly after, the path zig-zags back left (east) then forks right (south-west) down into forest. At the Chaleyre Chalet, keep right (the left fork descends to Le Tour) and, despite some twists and turns, stay in a south-west direction until not far above the N506 road. The path veers parallel to the road (north-west then north) and joins a track near car parking up to **Col des Montets** (1461m – 4793ft).

The Aiguilles Rouges Nature Reserve Interpretation Centre contains exhibitions, an audio-visual display, books and leaflets for sale and a bar. Several kilometres of nature trail have been laid out on adjacent hillside, species are labelled and clearly a concerted effort is being made to interest visitors in what the neighbouring habitats contain and to generate respect for the wild life.

Our route now takes to the old road opposite the Centre (now used for car parking) and about 150m after rejoining the main road forks right down a track across Les Planards, a swath of rough, scrubby land used for unofficial wild camping. From now on, you keep company with the infant Eau Noire torrent and the railway line (which emerges from the Montroc Tunnel) all the way to **Le Buet**. Here, keep forward, close to the railway at Les Montets (ignore paths off right to a rock-climbing crag) and simply shadow the railway line, picking up a good track past a holiday centre back to the Hôtel des Voyageurs. Turn left over the line to the station car park.

## Walk 3   The Tré-Les-Eaux Valley

Routing: Le Couteray – Les Granges – Tré-les-Eaux valley – Les
         Granges – Sur le Rocher – Le Couteray.
Total ascent: 640m (2100ft)
Timings: Ascent 3 hours; descent 2½ hours.
No refreshment point.
*Special note: There is some simple rock scrambling in a few places,
and possible snowbanks to cross early in the season in the valley's
upper reaches.*

The two great attractions of this walk are its relative seclusion and the
wonderful alpine flora to be found, especially in the lower section.
Tucked away near the Swiss border and with no refuge or spectacular
viewpoint to draw large numbers of walkers to it, the Tré-les-Eaux
valley exudes a romantic, almost Wagnerian splendour rarely
encountered elsewhere in this popular region of the Alps.

Descending on the N506 road north from Col des Montets, cross
the Eau Noire torrent just past Le Buet S.N.C.F. station and take the
next turning left up to **Le Couteray**. There are a couple of good
parking lay-bys.

Past the 2nd hairpin bend, turn off right at a sign for 'Loriaz' (this is
an alternative start to the Refuge de Loriaz, see Walk 1) and a 'Sauf
Riverains' road sign (no entry except for access). This good track
runs up to Les Granges. At the first corner and a clearer Refuge de
Loriaz sign, take a footpath off left, short-cutting a big dog-leg bend
in the track. It leads up across luxuriant grassy hillside towards the
high rocky pyramid of Aiguille de Loriaz (2752m – 9029ft). Keep
ahead at a path junction and when the track is rejoined turn left.
Take another short-cut path off left and turn left again onto the track,
passing a path to Sur le Rocher.

Continue up the track and soon, half way along a straight stretch,
watch for a sign 'Tré-les-Eaux' pointing left; this path doubles back
and is waymarked with a No. 6 symbol. **Les Granges** is a cluster of
idyllic old chalets set on a beautiful south-facing shelf of wooded
mountainside. Stay on the right-hand, level path, passing a turning
left to 'Sur le Rocher' beyond the last chalet (this path is taken on the
descent.)

Climbing gently over bouldery slopes in and out of trees, you will
be walking through drifts of colourful wild flowers, especially if the

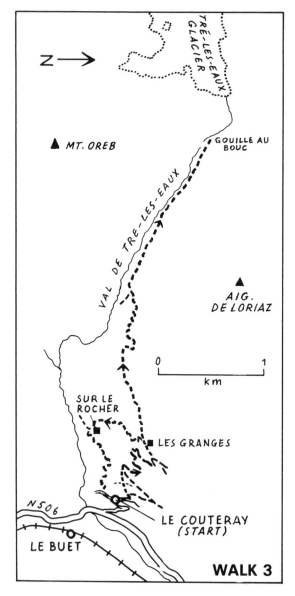

summer is still young; their profusion is quite exceptional. Indeed, beyond a water outlet the surroundings resemble a well stocked rock garden and a large number of species is represented, among them rock jasmine, pasque flowers and saxifrage.

The way crosses coarse scree and rises still towards the shattered rock pyramid of **Aiguille de Loriaz**. Soon there is a steepening of gradient and a hardening underfoot until a massive boulder is reached, signifying the start of a determined climb up stony slopes beneath rock buttresses, across boulders and up an easy-angled rocky groove.

More exciting now, the path leads airily above rocky bluffs and rises to a corner. Here is the first sight ahead into the steep-sided ravine of **Val de Tré-les-Eaux**. Equally compelling is the view back to the Tour and Argentière glaciers. Held on a ledge between orange-stained cliffs above and precipices plunging down to the unseen ravine bed, the path edges along to an open shoulder and begins to drop towards a line of inclined cliffs ahead.

Down at this leveller, grassy passage, a path comes in from the left (a less well defined and technically more difficult route up from Le Buet, not recommended as a descent for walkers owing to exposed and awkward rock pitches.)

The final section of this walk now takes an undulating line north-west over mixed terrain along the containing valley sides, but still some way above the torrent for the most part. There is another easy rock stretch to negotiate, but the principal preoccupation will doubtless be with appreciating the increasingly wild recesses of this unique valley with its stands of pines and snow streaked headwall.

The finale is reached (over possible snowbanks) at **Gouille au Bouc** (Gully of the Goat 1990m – 6529ft) where the torrent from Tré-les-Eaux Glacier up to the west emerges steeply from the mouth of a gorge. Actually, it is possible to climb further, heading left onto the moraine for a closer view of the glacier, but there is no path as such and this must be left to the discretion of individual walkers.

Return by the same route as far as the approaches to Les Granges hamlet. About 20m before the first chalet, turn sharp right, signed 'Sur le Rocher'. The path meanders very pleasantly along through pine forest, crosses a brook then a torrent (Ruisseau de la Meunière) on a log bridge. At a path intersection, keep right, down by an irrigation channel and emerge at a clearing with chalets – **Sur le Rocher**.

Walk straight ahead between the lower chalets and descend into a small, luxuriantly vegetated rocky ravine. Ignore one thin path off

*In the wild Tré-les-Eaux valley*

left and, farther down, another one. You soon come to a clearing with the Meunière torrent cascading below. The path drops to stream level and reaches chalets; cross a meadow and, arriving at the road, turn left into Le Couteray and back to the start.

## Walk 4   The Pierre à Bérard Refuge and Col de Salenton

Routing: Le Buet – La Poya – Cascade du Bérard – l'Eau Bérard
         valley – Pierre à Bérard Refuge – Col de Salenton. Return
         by same route.

Total ascent: 1189m (3901ft)

Timings: Le Buet to Pierre à Bérard Refuge – 2 hours
         Refuge to Col de Salenton – 2 hours
         Descent to refuge – 1 hour
         Descent from refuge to Le Buet – 1¼ hours

Meals, drinks and accommodation available at the Pierre à Bérard Refuge. Snacks and drinks at 'La Cascade' buvette.

*Special note: Although the ascent to the Pierre à Bérard Refuge is easy, the subsequent climb to Col de Salenton is much more rugged and may be snow covered in its upper reaches early in the summer when an ice-axe will be useful. Obtaining a weather prediction is advisable if it is intended to continue above the refuge.*

This walk divides itself into two distinct parts. Reaching the Pierre à Bérard Refuge is one of the easiest routes in this guide, but although for this reason you are likely to meet numerous fellow walkers of all ages on the path, it is a rewarding excursion in its own right, with the unusual little refuge as your destination. Mountaineers use it too as a stepping stone for an ascent of Mont Buet, considered by some guides to be an ideal 'dry run' for their clients before attempting Mont Blanc itself. The second part of the route to Col de Salenton calls for a change of gear as gradients steepen and surroundings become increasingly wild.

**Le Buet** is a small hamlet straddling the N506 north of Col des Montets. The walk begins from the S.N.C.F. railway station car park adjacent to the Hôtel du Buet. Take the path on the opposite side of the road, signed to Mont Buet and Cascade de Bérard. Crossing bouldery meadow, the impressive rock pyramid of Aiguille de Loriaz (2752m – 8438ft) looms ahead. **La Poya's** old chalets – all weathered stone and timber – display the beauty intrinsic in natural materials used in traditional ways. There are good views back south-east to Aiguille des Grands Montets (3295m – 10,810ft).

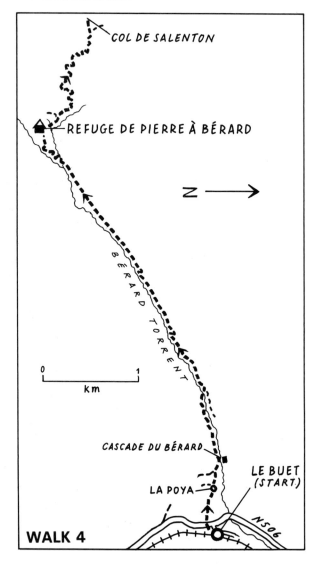

COL DE SALENTON

REFUGE DE PIERRE À BÉRARD

N →

BÉRARD TORRENT

0        1
km

CASCADE DU BÉRARD

LE BUET
(START)

LA POYA

N506

WALK 4

*Chalets at La Poya. Aiguille de Loriaz centre top.*

*The trail to the Pierre à Bérard Refuge and Col de Salenton*

Reaching a path junction soon in woods, take the right fork; a viewpoint on the right gives a first glimpse of the Bérard torrent, rushing below in its gorge. Follow the path above a wooden bridge to a waymarked boulder and in a short distance you come out opposite **'La Cascade' buvette** (snacks/drinks), its terrace built over a jumble of massive boulders jammed into the torrent bed.

Unless refreshments are already required, keep ahead on the rocky path which climbs gently along above the Eau Bérard in a delightful, unspoilt valley setting amongst larch trees, wild flowers and a chaos of rocks. Notices warn of sudden fluctuations in water level due to hydro-electric flow controls. Near its source, the torrent is, in fact, connected by subterranean pipe to the great Émosson reservoirs to the north and the author can vouch for the necessity for warning signs: on one occasion, a surge of brown foaming water considerably raised the torrent's level and turbulence, creating a potential hazard along its immediate banks.

A path from Le Couteray via Sur le Rocher – an alternative start – comes in over a footbridge by some benches. This leveller stretch is the first of two plateaux encountered on the walk in the Vallon de Bérard. In about 200m the torrent is crossed on a log bridge – Pont de la Vordette – whereafter increasingly sparse forest slowly reveals the snow streaked mountain slopes at the valley head.

More gradual ascent, path and torrent both punctuated by many huge boulders, leads to an abrupt levelling off as the second plateau is reached. A line of low cliffs is passed by zig-zags and then it's flat walking for a while, the Pierre à Bérard Refuge just discernible ahead. Approaching it, the path mounts rougher slopes, crosses a feeder stream and the refuge is lost from sight behind steeper hummocky ground and banks of alpenrose. A few twists and turns and the way is clear up to the **Pierre à Bérard Refuge** (1924m – 6312ft. Privately owned; 30 places; open during the summer. Meals, drinks, snacks.)

The building is protected from avalanche by a monolithic rock, against which it huddles and from which it takes its name. Though small and very popular, the hut's dark, simple interior has managed to retain an authentic, almost timeless ambience.

Nearby, a yellow sign indicates directions to col de Bérard (2460m – 8071ft) reached up a permanent snowfield to the south-west, and to Col de Salenton, the ultimate objective of this route. Our path zig-zags to the right (north-west) of the refuge towards a 'Prise d'Eau' (water supply installation) and a rugged confusion of rock and grass. Altitude is gained relentlessly on stony mountainside strewn with large rocks and the way, indicated by paint flashes, is not always clear on the ground. A general direction of west-north-west is maintained, however, crossing probable snowbanks, until the col itself is approached with Aiguille de Salenton ahead.

In fact, the ascent route to Mont Buet angles off to the north from here, but keep left, still following the odd waymarking and climb steeply to the saddle. **Col de Salenton** (2526m – 8287ft) is an impressive situation, very steep on its western side, and stands on the perimeter of the Aiguilles Rouges Nature Reserve (Interpretation Centre by the road on Col des Montets). It is also an important walkers' link between the easternmost mountains and valleys of this part of the French Alps leading to the Swiss border, and the Diosaz valley which drops past Col d'Anterne to Servoz, west of Chamonix. (This traverse forms part of the Tour des Aiguilles Rouges – see Walk 5).

Return to Le Buet is by the same route used for the ascent.

## Walk 5    Tour of the Aiguilles Rouges

Routing: *Day 1* Le Buet village – Pierre à Bérard Refuge – Col de Salenton – Chalets de Villy – Chalet-hôtel Moëde-Anterne

*Day 2* Chalet-hôtel Moëde-Anterne – Pont d'Arlevé – Col du Brévent – Planpraz – La Flégère Refuge

*Day 3* La Flégère Refuge – Chalet des Chéserys (variant via Lac Blanc) – Col des Montets – Le Buet village

Total ascent: *Day 1* – 1366m (4482ft)

*Day 2* – 771m (2529ft)

*Day 3* – 183m (600ft); Variant – 971m (3186ft)

Timings: *Day 1* Le Buet to the Pierre à Bérard Refuge – 2 hours

Pierre à Bérard Refuge to Col de Salenton – 2 hours

Col de Salenton to Chalets de Villy – 1½ hours

Chalets de Villy to Chalet-hôtel Moëde-Anterne – 2 hours

*Day 2* Chalet-hôtel Moëde-Anterne to Pont d'Arlevé – 1 hour

Pont d'Arlevé to Col du Brévent – 2¼ hours

Col du Brévent to Planpraz – 1 hour

Planpraz to La Flégère Refuge – 1¾ hours

*Day 3* La Flégère Refuge to Chalet des Chéserys – 1¼ hours (or 2½ hours via Lac Blanc)

Chalets des Chéserys to Col des Montets – 1¾ hours

Col des Montets to Le Buet ¾ hour

Availability of meals, drinks and accommodation:

*Day 1* Le Buet village, Pierre à Bérard Refuge, Chalets de Villy (basic shelter only), Chalet-hôtel Moëde-Anterne

*Day 2* Planpraz (no accom.), La Flégère Refuge

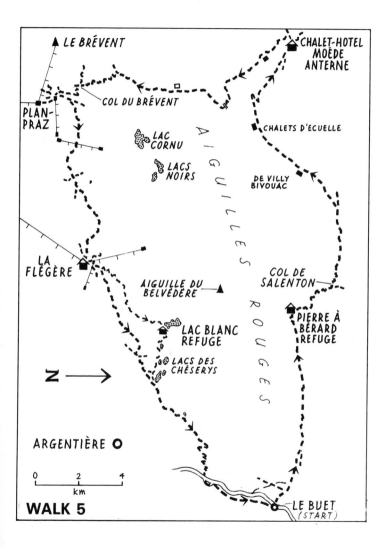

LE BRÉVENT

CHALET-HOTEL
MOÈDE
ANTERNE

COL DU BRÉVENT

PLAN-
PRAZ

CHALETS D'ECUELLE

LAC
CORNU

A I G U I L L E S

LACS
NOIRS

DE VILLY
BIVOUAC

LA
FLÉGÈRE

AIGUILLE DU
BELVÉDÈRE

COL DE
SALENTON

R O U G E S

PIERRE À
BÉRARD
REFUGE

LAC BLANC
REFUGE

N →

LACS DES
CHÉSERYS

ARGENTIÈRE O

0    2    4
km

WALK 5

LE BUET
(START)

61

> *Day 3* Col des Montets (no accom.); Lac Blanc Refuge (no accom.)

*Special note: This 3-day expedition could be compressed into 2 by combining Days 2 and 3 which are, in any case, considerably easier. Conditions underfoot will depend very much on the time of year; early summer may see extensive snow cover on the higher stretches of trail, particularly Col de Salenton (very steep and needing extreme care when snowed up) and Col du Brévent. At such times it is advisable to carry an ice-axe in addition to good sunglasses or snow goggles, suncream and warm clothing. Otherwise, paths are generally good throughout, though always rugged.*

*Advance booking at refuges is strongly recommended during July and August. There is plenty of scope for lightweight campers to pitch wild, but it is always necessary to be discreet (eg. Pitching well away from popular paths) and to leave no litter.*

*A spell of reasonably fine weather, though not guaranteed on a visit of limited duration, will greatly increase enjoyment of this splendid route. Unless an improvement is forecast, it is unwise to set off in poor conditions, since the first day's itinerary is serious and the Col de Salenton no piece of cake in mist, rain and wind. Once over the col however, there are various escape routes from subsequent high ground should circumstances suggest a retreat.*

The **Aiguiles Rouges** massif forms a counterpoint, albeit of more modest dimensions, to the great wall of mountains and glaciers on the other side of the Chamonix valley. It is a spine of rocky summits running roughly north-east to south-west and culminating in Mont Buet (3096m – 10,157ft), which stands about 5km west of Le Buet village where the tour begins.

It is fine rough-walking country and a scattering of mountain refuges makes this route as feasible for the hut-hopper as it unquestionably is for the backpacker. Because it is circular, the walk can be started from any convenient point and followed in either direction; it is, however, important to plan overnight stops realistically.

Covering the 35km (22 miles) in 3 days will not unduly tax the mountain walker who is moderately fit and who has map and compass skills should the weather close in. Attempting the tour in 2 days is more ambitious but well within the range of the fit and able.

In order to give priority to route directions, view descriptions etc. are kept to the minimum. For more detailed notes about sections of trail (except Col de Salenton to Col du Brévent), please refer to the relevant Day Walks elsewhere in this guide.

## DAY 1

**Le Buet** straddles the N506 road north of Col des Montets and the tour starts from its railway station car park adjacent to the Hôtel du Buet. Cross the road and follow the well signed path for the Cascade de Bérard and Mont Buet. Beyond the ancient chalets of La Poya, keep right at a junction in woods and you soon come up opposite **'La Cascade' buvette** (snacks, drinks) and the Bérard torrent.

Keep ahead on the rocky path, climbing gently by the Eau Bérard in a charming, unspoilt valley setting. This level stretch is one of two plateaux on the ascent to the Pierre à Bérard Refuge. The way crosses the torrent and reaches thinner forest where views open out ahead for the first time towards the snow-streaked Aiguille de Bérard. The second plateau is reached and after some short zig-zags above low cliffs, there is flat walking for a while.

Towards the refuge, rougher slopes are climbed but the path is clear and well walked, crossing feeder streams and arriving at the **Pierre à Bérard Refuge** (1924m – 6312ft; privately owned; 30 places; open during the summer; meals, snacks and drinks). The building huddles beneath a monolithic rock which protects it from avalanches and gives it its name. Easily accessible to walkers of all ages and abilities, the refuge nevertheless remains simple and refreshingly authentic.

A nearby yellow sign points in the direction of Col de Salenton and the thinner path zig-zags to the right (north-west) towards a water supply installation and a rugged confusion of rock and grass. The climbing becomes quite tough and unremitting as altitude is gained rapidly. Occasional paint flashes mark a tortuous way (not always clear) over wild, rock-strewn mountainside. Keeping generally west-north-west and crossing probable snowbanks, a final pull up left from the junction with the Mont Buet path brings you to **Col de Salenton** (2526m – 8287ft) at the conjunction of the Aiguilles Rouges and Passy Nature Reserves.

The narrow saddle is an impressive place at which to linger, but a good deal of walking still remains to be done to conclude this first day. Great care is needed on the descent west, which is initially very steep down a small combe. In snowy or icy conditions, every precaution must be taken to avoid a fall. Soon, however, gradient and terrain grow gentler as the path (scantily waymarked) enters the valley system of the Diosaz torrent which runs through gorges lower down near its confluence with the River Arve at Servoz.

Veering south-west, you traverse a steep-sided knoll, cross a feeder stream then La Diosaz torrent itself where numerous rivulets and gullies drain down from Tête de Villy up to the west. A path junction is soon reached: either fork leads onwards to the Chalet-hôtel Moëde-Anterne, but the lower, left, path is somewhat easier and passes **Chalets de Villy** (1885m – 6184ft) where there is the possibility of shelter (unguarded bivouac).

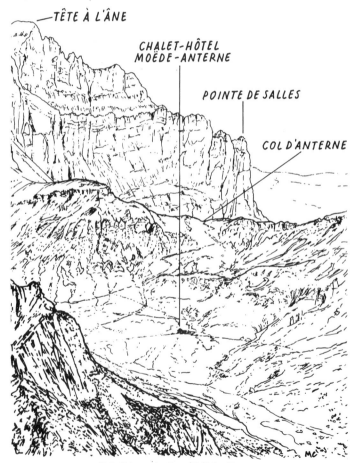

TÊTE À L'ÂNE

CHALET-HÔTEL
MOËDE-ANTERNE

POINTE DE SALLES

COL D'ANTERNE

*Col d'Anterne from Col du Brévent*

An ancient way over rough pasture now climbs south, crossing stream beds and another major feeder of the Diosaz – Ruisseau d'Écuelle – at the ruinous **Chalets d'Écuelle** (1904m – 6247ft). Still rising along steep hillside beneath cliff and scree, Collet d'Écuelle is reached, a rocky shoulder facing Pointe Noire de Pormenaz. Here you swing right (west), contouring over mixed terrain to the **Chalet-hôtel Moëde-Anterne** (2002m – 6568ft; privately owned; 60 places; resident guardian from beginning July to mid-Sept; reservations tel: 93.60.43; meals, snacks, drinks).

DAY 2

A good track (the routing for the long-distance GR5 Grand Traverse of the Alps) descends first south-west then back east above the small Laouchet lake, passing below the Chalets de Moëde and yesterday's higher path and following down the left bank of the Moëde torrent amidst a profusion of wild flowers. Rounding the Tête de Jeubon, the route turns down left (north-east) to reach **Pont d'Arlevé** (1597m – 5239ft), a small footbridge installed for each summer season.

Red and white GR5 waymarks lead on south as you climb along dry, bushy slopes before crossing a region of many torrents draining the Cornu and Noirs lakes above. You pass the ruined **Chalets d'Arlevé** (possible rough shelter) and in just over 1km reach a path junction (not shown on some maps). Keep left here, mounting increasingly steep and rocky slopes on a superbly graded path which takes you economically up through boulders and over probable snow to **Col du Brévent** (2368m – 7769ft).

Topping the snowy saddle of the col itself is one of the tour's magic moments, for quite suddenly a stupendous view is thrust upon you which, until this moment, was totally obscured by the high Brévent ridge. The transition from watching your own feet trudging up stony ground to a dazzling panorama of glaciated peaks above the Chamonix valley abyss is breathtaking.

NOTE: Le Brévent summit (2526m – 8287ft; cable-car to Planpraz) is an hour's walk/scramble to the south-west and could be included in the itinerary, adding the option of an overnight stay at the Bellachat Refuge (¾ hour beyond) and retracing steps on the morrow. For details of this stretch, please refer to Walk 11.

Zig-zags down over rock and snow follow the clear exit south-east from the col. Watch for an abrupt turn right (south-south-east) at a path junction, leading down a long steep slope, often snow covered and requiring care, especially early in the season. Ski-lift pylons announce the approaches to **Planpraz** and the 'Altitude 2000' bar/restaurant is soon in sight. (A cabin-lift desends direct to Chamonix from a little further down).

The final leg of Day 2 lies along the **Grand Balcon Sud** trail (also the Tour du Mont Blanc routing – red and white waymarks) to La Flégère. Where the path from Col du Brévent drops to a flatter bare area of pistes, turn down sharp left (north) under ski-lifts and keep to the lower trail ahead. After an initial loss of height, it undulates along rugged slopes, past the ruined Charlanon and Glière chalets, eventually encountering the top edge of forest and rising to **La Flégère Refuge** in the cable-car station building (1877m – 6158ft; privately owned; 100 places; guardian from June to Sept, closed in winter; reservations tel: (50) 53.06.13; meals, snacks and drinks; cable-car to Les Praz de Chamonix).

DAY 3

From the viewing table at La Flégère there is every chance to identify the array of glaciers and summits in the Chamonix Aiguilles opposite. Leave on the Tour du Mont Blanc routing north, pass beneath a ski-lift and ignore a fork right, to the valley. (The track up left from La Chavanne sheepfold building leads to Lac Blanc.)

NOTE: Although involving more ascent than the 'balcon' path, Lac Blanc and its refuge are spectacularly situated, and provided conditions are favourable can form an excellent variant to the onward route. The 'balcon' path can be joined farther on via the Chéserys lakes. For details of this itinerary, please refer to Walks 13 and 14.

Continuing forward (north-east) along Montagne de la Flégère, an exposed corner or two are encountered before the path crosses several small streams issuing from Lac Blanc above and reaches the **Chalet des Chéserys** (1998m – 6555ft). Just beyond the building, turn left (north-east), still on the Grand Balcon Sud/Tour du Mont Blanc, and in 750m come to a path intersection and a large waymarked cairn.

To the right is the main TMB routing over the 'passage délicat' on Aiguillette d'Argentière and thence down to Tré-le-Champ. Our direction remains north-east however, on the higher path passing a turning left from the Chéserys lakes and Lac Blanc – the variant mentioned above. A stony path takes you on past a small lake below tiered, green-hued slabs soaring towards rock summits around Aiguille Martin.

Beyond a final shoulder of land – La Remuaz – the Grand Balcon Sud fizzles out and the way descends on many tight zig-zags and round rocky corners to the Aiguilles Rouges Nature Reserve

Interpretation Centre on **Col des Montets** (1461m – 4793ft; exhibition, audio-visual display, books and leaflets for sale, bar).

Opposite the centre, an old road loop (now car parking) avoids a walk on the busy N506, except for the last 150m before a turning off right down a stony track across Les Planards, rough ground used for unofficial wild camping. From now on you keep close company with the infant Eau Noire torrent and the railway, after it has emerged from the Montroc Tunnel. Cross the line at **Le Buet** to return to the start.

### Suggested shorter walks in the Vallorcine area

THE TÊTE DE PRAZ TORRENT
Total ascent: 613m (2011ft) – 3¼ hours walking

From Le Buet railway station car park, cross the N506 and take the path opposite towards the Cascade de Bérard. Walk through La Poya hamlet and fork right in the woods ahead. Shortly before reaching the buvette, turn left on a track towards a ski-lift but before passing beneath it, fork right. The rising path crosses ski pistes in the Forêt de la Ravine, traverses bushy slopes, stream beds and a couloir and veers right (west) to climb the crest of an old moraine alongside the Tête de Praz torrent. (1950m – 6398ft.).

There are many rock climbing routes on the cliffs of Aiguilles de Praz-Torrent ahead, while to the east are magnificent views over Argentière and across to Le Tour Glacier.

LE CHÂTELARD, THE SWISS FRONTIER AND CASCADE DU DARD
Total ascent: 98m (322ft) – 2½ hours walking

There is a large car park at Vallorcine railway station. Start the walk north-east on a track from the car park, parallel to the railway. Cross the line and follow the track left; in some 500m this becomes a path alongside the railway, Eau Noire torrent and N506 road, squeezed together in this narrow neck of wooded valley. The road is finally joined near Pont de l'Ile beyond an Oratory. Ahead lies the Swiss frontier and customs buildings and to the right the large turbine hall producing electricity from water released through the big Émosson dam high above to the north-west (see Walk 1).

100m or so back along the main road, turn off right on a lane to Barberine, crossing the Eau Noire. At the top of the village, continue north-west on a path up through pine forest. Reaching a path intersection, it is only a short distance right (signed) to the Cascade du Dard. Retrace steps to the junction and go down right (south-east) on a sometimes bouldery path passing a ruined chalet, crossing the Nant du Rand and emerging at the road-end at Le Molard hamlet. Now simply keep forward past Le Clos church and Le Siseray, turn right along the N506 in Vallorcine and left back to the S.N.C.F. station.

## REFUGE DE LORIAZ
Total ascent: 720m (2362ft) – 3¾ hours walking

Le Nant/Le Morzay is a village mid-way between Le Buet and Vallorcine. There is limited parking on side roads. A path leaves north-west alongside the Loriaz stream, climbing above the chalets and veering away south-west after 500m onto a track in forest. Joining the jeep-track from Le Couteray, follow its hairpin bends and watch for a fork off right (north-east) into forest. This crosses the Loriaz stream valley and thereafter ascends in a series of zig-zags to emerge above the treeline on a broad sloping plateau. Near the conspicuous Loriaz cross, the path from Le Crot is joined, and a little more climbing brings you up to the Refuge de Loriaz (for details see Walk 1).

Return by the same route, or take the Le Crot path down to the valley and follow a roadside track back to Le Nan (add ½ hour).

*European Larch*

# 2:
# The Argentière Area

*Mont Buet (top centre) from the trail to the*
*Albert Premier Refuge*

## Walk 6 Col de Balme and Source of the River Arve

Routing: Le Tour – Chalets de Charamillon – Col de Balme – Tête de
Balme – Col des Posettes – Ardoissières – Le Tour

Total ascent: 946m (3104ft)

Timings: Ascent to Tête de Balme – 2¾ hours
Descent via Ardoissières – 2½ hours

Meals, snacks, drinks and accommodation available at the Col de
Balme Refuge.

For a note about the village of Le Tour, please see the start of Walk 7.
The River Arve – such a distinctive feature of the Chamonix valley as
it hurries down, grey-green with meltwater and glacial silt under a
haze of condensing vapour – rises close to Col de Balme. Not only is
this saddle a watershed at the north-eastern extremity of the
Chamonix valley, but it is on the Swiss frontier too. Winter skiing and
tourism have largely supplanted farming in this high, snow-prone
valley head, though cattle are still grazed here and there.

The Col de Balme Refuge is a popular one, at the axial point of
several routes and introducing walkers on the long-distance Tour du
Mont Blanc to their final stage. Tête de Balme is no great distance or
height from the col, but provides splendid views which encompass
little Lac de Catogne and peaks to the north-east. This walk actually
encircles the Arve's headwaters and because your line of sight is
angled south-west, the whole group of summits and glaciers which
make up the Mont Blanc massif are a constant and majestic focus.

From the northern end of **Le Tour** (large car park, grocery store,
bars/restaurants; Refuge du Tour, Club Alpin Français, 60 places,
open all year, resident guardian, reservations tel. 54.04.16) follow
the stony track climbing between the Arve torrent and the
telecabin/ski-lift. (This is waymarked red and white, being on the
Tour du Mont Blanc). In about 750m, the path zig-zags beneath the
lift cables, thereafter keeping in their general direction (north-north-
east). The gradient eases and soon the intermediate telecabin station
is reached at **Chalets de Charamillon** (1760m – 5774ft).

Keep left (north) on a good track which crosses a small valley near
the confluence of the Charamillon and Carlavé torrents. Just the
other side, fork right (north-east) on a well-walked path leading
directly up easy slopes, under a ski-lift to **Col de Balme** (2191m
7188ft). The popular refuge (privately owned, 25 places, resident
guardian, open all year, meals, snacks, drinks), with its bright paint
and cool, shady interior, has considerable charm. To the north-east,

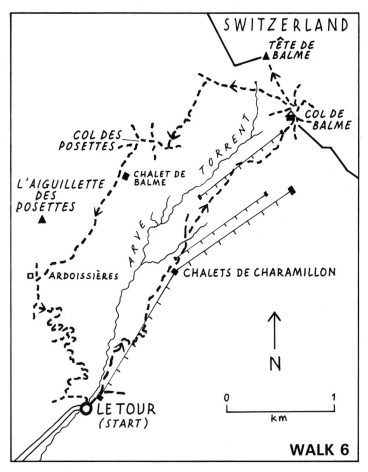

the Nant Noir valley falls away into Switzerland and both the main paths in view are on the Tour du Mont Blanc, the higher right-hand one being a variant from the Trient Glacier, out of sight to the east.

Leave the refuge's terrace on a path descending right (north) to a signpost and turn left towards Col des Posettes. Instead of continuing along the path (although this is, in fact, our onward route), strike up right (north-west), following the grassy ridge line for about 500m and

*Col de Balme Refuge. Aiguille Verte and the Drus (left), Chamonix Aiguilles distant centre.*

130m (427ft) of climbing to reach the **Tête de Balme** viewpoint (2321m – 7615ft). In good visibility, there are few places at this altitude which offer a better panorama. In addition to the great vista of Mont Blanc and the Chamonix valley, there is more local interest in the form of the Arolette crucifix just to the north-east, and Lac de Catogne set in its shallow basin surrounded by small rocky outcrops.

Descend back to the path and follow it down (generally west-south-west) over grassy mountainside. The source of the River Arve lies a short way up north and there are exceptional views of the Le Tour Glacier and Chamonix Aiguilles. Beyond a path junction, you reach the flat, almost plateau-like **Col des Posettes** (1997m – 6552ft). Still on a Tour du Mont Blanc variant, turn left (south-west), waymarked for Ardoissières. (In 150m, the path rising right traverses the Aiguillette des Posettes ridge and could form an alternative route to Ardoissières; allow an extra ½ hour and refer to Walk 2).

Climbing gently, the clear path passes above the wooden shingled barns and their herd of cows at **Chalet de Balme**. The slopes above and below are carpeted with myrtle and dwarf alpenrose as height is very gradually gained to where a path from the Aiguillette des Posettes ridge comes down from the right near the abandoned **Ardoissières** chalets.

Here we begin the descent proper to Le Tour by turning left (south). Turn left off the Tour du Mont Blanc (which continues towards Tré-le-Champ) and proceed on down innumerable zig-zags, past marvellous banks of wild flowers. The path eventually swings right, down through trees and the final zig-zags lead out to a small meadow. Keep left to cross the infant Arve and return to the car park in Le Tour.

### Walk 7   The Albert Premier Refuge

Routing: Le Tour – Chalets de Charamillon – Combe de Vormaine – Bec du Picheu – Albert Premier Refuge. Return by same route (or extension via Lac de Charamillon to top station of telecabin, using it to descend to Le Tour. During the ascent or descent, optional use can be made of the telecabin between Le Tour and Chalets de Charamillon.)

Total ascent; 1232m (4042ft)

Timings: Ascent 3½ hours, descent 2 hours.

Meals, drinks and accommodation available at the Albert Premier Refuge.

*Special note: This route climbs into a high mountain environment. It is advisable to obtain a weather forecast before deciding to set out, and to go prepared. In addition to the usual gear, this means taking warm clothing, suncream and sunhat, snow goggles or good sunglasses and an ice axe. Early in the season (from mid-June), crampons might also be needed.*

Walks 6 and 7 begin at Le Tour, a traditional Savoyard village situated 4km north-east of Argentière. It receives more winter snowfall than anywhere else in France – as much as 5m (16ft) in depth – and the surrounding slopes are popular with skiers. The village is inextricably associated with Michel Croz, an inhabitant who was to become a celebrated guide and who led Edward Whymper to the summits of the Aiguille Verte and the Matterhorn but died during the descent of the latter.

Given favourable conditions, this route provides a marvellous opportunity for walkers to enter the domain of the high altitude mountaineer, yet presents no undue technical difficulty. From the start, there are extensive views down the Chamonix valley to the shining summits of the Mont Blanc massif. The refuge is perched on a rocky spur above the Glacier du Tour, from which are ranged the serrated, snow-streaked tops of the Aiguilles Rouges and Mont Buet.

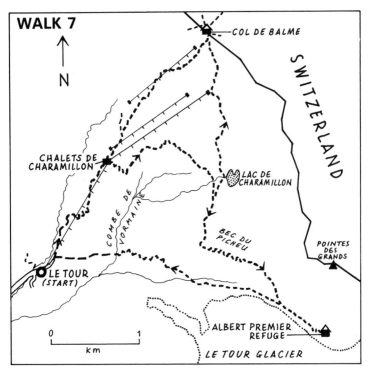

At the northern end of **Le Tour** (large car park, grocery store, bars/restaurants), take to the stony, much used track (waymarked red and white, part of the Tour du Mont Blanc long-distance trail) which climbs at first between the telecabin/ski lift and the Arve torrent. The path eventually zig-zags beneath the lift, but always keeps to its general direction (north-north-east). Less steep ground is reached at Plan du Caiset and soon the path arrives at the intermediate telecabin station at **Chalets de Charamillon.** Here turn right (east) on a narrower path (waymarked to Albert Premier) which climbs round the head of the vast **Combe de Vormaine**. From this section of path, the Chamonix valley and Mont Blanc are distant enough to be seen in an overall perspective, almost end-on.

Reaching a flatter, marshy plateau, the best path keeps to the right of a conspicuous rain guage and doubles back to an iron post, at

*On the trail to the Albert Premier Refuge (early season):*
*Aiguille du Chardonnet top right*

which turn right. Cross the torrent draining Lac de Charamillon above (which can be entertaining early in the summer when in spate with meltwater!) and pass a path junction. (Left leads back to the telecabin top station and Col de Balme, an optional extension on the return leg.)

The route now slants up over rugged slopes (steep snow patches early in the season) and rounds a rocky shoulder beneath **Bec du Picheu** to reveal a sudden and breathtaking panorama over the **Glacier du Tour** and **Aiguille du Chardonnet**. Winding on round rough hillside, the path climbs in zig-zags and soon the refuge is visible ahead, a square-cut profile on a bastion of rock near the head of the ice-fall.

A short descent is made to negotiate rocky steps and a gully equipped with fixed metal rails (mainly useful in very early season when snow and ice may cover the path), whereafter coarse scree and stones interspersed with snowbanks are traversed to a spine of moraine adjacent to the glacier. After late or heavy spring snows, this entire basin remains an extensive snowfield until well into the summer. Fortunately, gradients are not particularly steep and normal ice-axe safeguarding is all that is required; in freezing conditions, however, crampons would be necessary.

*Le Tour Glacier and Aiguilles Rouges from the Albert Premier Refuge*

Continue up the moraine and tackle the final steeper climb, either over barren rocks, shale and mud, or up a zig-zag track stamped in snow, depending on conditions. A scramble up the last boulders leads to the **Albert Premier Refuge** (2702m – 8865ft. Club Alpin Français; 128 places; guardian from the beginning of June to the end of September; 40 places in winter. Meals, drinks, snacks; reservations tel: 54.06.20).

The refuge's name is a memorial to King Albert 1st of Belgium, a highly accomplished alpinist and member of Club Alpin Français, who was killed whilst abseiling in the Ardennes in 1934. Views west from the terrace are exceptionally fine, taking in the Aiguilles Rouges, Mont Buet and Grand Mont-Ruan, while immediately below the Glacier du Tour falls away to the unseen depths of the Chamonix valley.

Snow slopes lead on above the refuge buildings to the frontier ridge with Switzerland, and there are mountaineering routes south and east out across the glacier, dominated here by the shapely pyramid of the Aiguille du Chardonnet (3824m – 12,546ft).

Take the same route back. (A possible, though less scenic, alternative follows the moraine right down beside the glacier, passes Fenêtre du Tour, crosses the Picheu torrent and climbs out the other side before dropping more steeply in rough zig-zags – care needed – to easy ground across les Granges on a good track back to Le Tour.) At the junction above the rain gauge, keep right; this will take you past **Lac de Charamillon** (frozen over except in high summer) and on along a good path to the telecabin top station. Before making the mechanised descent, it is only a 20min. stroll each way to the refuge on Col de Balme at the Swiss frontier (meals, drinks).

**Walk 8    Tête du Grand Chantet**
Routing: Le Planet – Forêt du Grand Chantet – Tête du Grand
         Chantet – Montagne de Peclerey – Petit Balcon Nord – Le
         Planet
Total ascent: 604m (1982ft)
Timings: Le Planet to Tête du Grand Chantet – 2 hours
         Descent via Petit Balcon Nord – 1½ hours

This shorter itinerary provides an excellent and varied easy day walk with exciting views of Le Tour Glacier, the upper reaches of the Arve valley and the Aiguilles Rouges massif. The climbing comes in two instalments – a forest section on easy gradients and a sharp 280m (920ft) pull up tight zig-zags. The circuit is equally rewarding in the

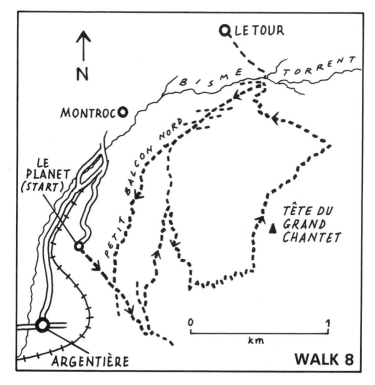

**WALK 8**

reverse direction.

**Le Planet** (1383m – 4537ft) is reached on a by-road south from Montroc, between Argentière and Le Tour. From the road-end close to the old Hôtel du Planet, a good path leaves south, climbing gently. Keep straight ahead at the first intersection (the path being crossed is the Petit Balcon Nord from Le Tour to Argentière) and at the next junction in larch forest just before a stream valley, turn sharp left (west then north). Height is gained gently in the **Forêt du Grand Chantet**, interrupted by the large Couloir du Grand Chantet.

At the ensuing path junction, close by a spring (spot height 1608m), turn back right (south), cross the couloir again, this time higher up, and gird up your loins for a sequence of steep zig-zags taking you out of forest to the head of the couloir at 1990m (6529ft).

500m over to the left (north) on a grassy alp stands a small shelter under the bulge of **Tête du Grand Chantet** and the higher Bec Rouge ridge.

In clear visibility this is a fine spot. To the west are ranged the Aiguilles Rouges, a wall of serrated, snow-streaked peaks, while to the north, mountainsides close in towards the source of the River Arve and the Swiss frontier (see Walk 6).

The way now drops over the initially stony slopes of **Montagne de Peclerey** and, before swinging left (north-west), provides stunning views of Le Tour Glacier, a broad swathe of contorted ice inclined steeply above the valley. More rugged descent leads down towards Le Tour village, but instead of crossing the Bisme torrent footbridge, turn sharp left on level ground at first (not the path beside the torrent itself), subsequently rising gently over stream beds, in and out of forest.

This is the **Petit Balcon Nord** to Argentière and we follow its pleasant meanderings for over 2km. Ignore a fork up left, dropping instead above Montroc and Les Frasserands. A few undulations later, you arrive at the path junction just above the start of the walk; Le Planet lies 300m down to the right.

## Walk 9   The Argentière Glacier
Routing: Les Chosalets – Plan Joran – La Croix de Lognan – Glacier d'Argentière viewpoint – Chalet Militaire de Lognan – Les Chosalets. (Croix de Lognan can be reached direct by cable-car)

Total ascent: 1118m (3668ft)

Timings: Les Chosalets to La Croix de Lognan – 2 hours
La Croix de Lognan to glacier viewpoint – 1 hour
Descent to Chalet Militaire – 30min.
Chalet Militaire to Les Chosalets – 1½ hours

Meals, snacks and drinks available at the Croix de Lognan cable-car station.

Each of the 10 or so glaciers accessible to walkers on the northern flanks of the Mont Blanc massif is more distinctly different from its neighbours than you would imagine to be likely. No doubt this is partly due to the varying qualities of the approach walks and the disposition of other features against which the glaciers are seen. However, this walk gets on intimate terms with the Argentière Glacier, a river of ice fed by a clutch of smaller glaciers and which stretches down from Mont Dolent to the south-east, rivalling Mer de

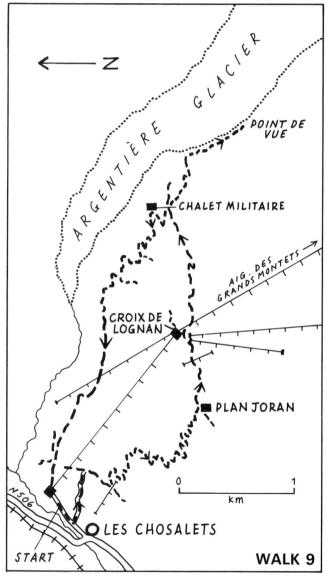

A R G E N T I È R E   G L A C I E R

POINT DE VUE

CHALET MILITAIRE

AIG. DES GRANDS MONTETS

CROIX DE LOGNAN

PLAN JORAN

0                    1
km

N 506

LES CHOSALETS

START

**WALK 9**

Glace for size in its upper reaches. Even though only encountering its lower, narrower section, the experience provides a graphic reminder of the enormous forces resulting from the slow but relentless fracturing of thousands of tons of ice as gravity pulls it down over steep ground.

For a more comprehensive look at the complicated topography in this part of the Chamonix valley, the 2nd stage cable-car can be taken from La Croix de Lognan up to Aiguille des Grands Montets (3233m – 10,607ft).

There is generous car parking (and a nearby campsite) at the cable-car bottom station, reached from **Les Chosalets**, 1½km south-west of Argentière. From the cable-car station, walk south-west for about 500m and turn left off the road up a lane between chalets (waymarked 'La Rosière, Petit Balcon Nord and Lognan'). There is limited parking space at the lane end, where turn right onto a track which begins to climb and passes beneath a ski lift at the edge of forest. Keep right (signed Lognan), descend for about 20m then turn up left (to Lognan and Pendant par la Trapette).

The path zig-zags fairly steeply at first, then settles down to a gentle, well graded ascent through mixed woodland, waymarked with paint flashes. (A junction right, signed 'Pendant 1hr' does not appear on maps). Continue ahead and after more zig-zags reach open woodland with good views now to Col des Montets and the Aiguilles Rouges.

As you approach new ski development, the path diverts left beneath the buildings, then up to them (future changes are possible here): this is **Plan Joran**, the size of its restaurant and terrace witness to the huge popularity of this area as a winter skiing resort. Turn left on the bulldozed track which has superseded the original path; it crosses the couloir de la Jeureuma and contours round to the intermediate cable-car station between the valley and Aiguille des Montets – **La Croix de Lognan** (1975m – 6480ft. Meals, snacks and drinks.)

The slopes adjacent to the buildings are festooned with ski-tows, lifts, pylons and pistes which, lacking a disguising mantle of snow, present a rather dreary face to the summer visitor. A little above, a signpost points out various directions, including Glacier d'Argentière Point de Vue 1 hour.

Walk up the broad E.D.F. track beneath the cable-car and a chair lift. It winds easily round rugged mountainside above the **Chalet Militaire de Lognan** below left (a refuge run by the French army). At

*The Aiguilles Rouges Massif from above Croix-de-Lognan (left)*

the corner ahead, somewhat uninhibited painted words on a boulder suggest that the 'Vue sur le glacier' is up to the right – 20min, and this is confirmed a little beyond by a sign at a pylon (2070m – 6791ft). Interestingly, we are on the route taken by mountaineers going up to the Argentière Refuge (which involves crossing the glacier higher up) as a base for climbs in the area.

The rough path short-cuts a long track dog-leg by slanting up over boulders and streams. Reaching level ground by a hydro-electric gallery, you are suddenly face to face with the **Argentière Glacier** and it is a stunning sight – a jumbled chaos of green ice contorted into cliffs, caves, crevasses and seracs on this its steepest gradient.

Just left of the gallery, the path continues up the moraine, along its crest or on snow beside it, until arriving at the **Point de Vue** (2338m – 7671ft). Not only is more of the glacier now revealed, but the great line of scree and cliffs opposite, rising to the Aiguille de Chardonnet and holding in the higher Le Tour Glacier, is immensely impressive. Behind to the south, rock, snowbanks and the Glacier des Rognans sweep up to the Aiguille des Grands Montets.

It is possible, given favourable conditions, to extend the walk some way towards the **Moraine des Rognans**, but this does lead into more serious terrain and involves traversing the edge of the glacier itself. Whether or not to continue must be left to the discretion of individual walkers.

*Confronting the Argentière Glacier*

Descend to the pylon at the track bend and take the path past the Chalet Militaire, zig-zagging down, crossing a piste and dropping in and out of forest. An improving track follows the Aillires torrent bed down under an E.D.F. cable-lift and out onto a lane leading to the cable-car station and car park.

**Walk 10   Argentière to Servoz – The Petit Balcon Sud**
Routing: Argentière – Les Tines – Chamonix – Merlet – Plan de la
        Cry – Montvauthier – Servoz
Total ascent: 672m (2205ft)
Timings: Argentière to Les Tines – 1¼ hours
        Les Tines to Chamonix – 2¼ hours
        Chamonix to Merlet – 2¼ hours
        Merlet to Servoz – 2 hours
Meals, snacks, drinks and accommodation available a short distance off-route in the valley between Argentière and Chamonix: thereafter at Merlet (no accom.)

Taken in its entirety, this route would make for a long day out, though for the most part on easy paths and often in forest. Any section can be chosen on its own, however, and there are good bus and train links to return to starting points. Some climbing is involved here and there, but height is maintained at around 1250m (4100ft). Established since 1967 by the Chamonix Commune in conjunction with the Forestry Authority, the main paths provide memorable panoramas of the Mont Blanc massif and the valley itself, despite their modest altitude.

The great attractions of this Petit Balcon Sud are its easy accessibility (from numerous points along its length), its inter-connection with most of the major ascents from the valley and a good many mid-height paths, plus its ambling, sheltered nature which makes it ideal for an easy day's stroll or a bad-weather hike. In the following text, emphasis is placed on route directions rather than view descriptions, since the latter forms a continuously changing backdrop.

300m down from **Argentière's** Tourist Information Office, a path takes off right (south-west) behind the railway bridge towards La Corne à Bouc woods, rising in forest above chalets and the railway track. Levelling off above Lioutre, you cross slopes which are avalanche-prone in winter and soon pass a line of rock-climbing crags on the right known as Les Plaques Bellin. From occasional clearings

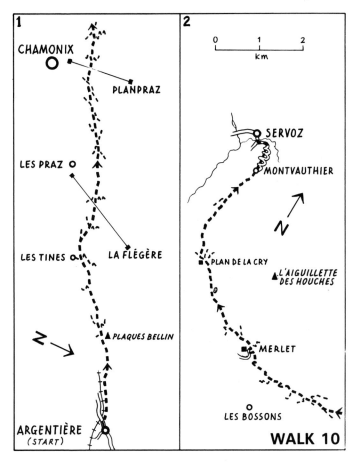

**1**

CHAMONIX ○

PLANPRAZ ■

LES PRAZ ○

▲

LES TINES ○

LA FLÉGÈRE

↖N→

▲ PLAQUES BELLIN

ARGENTIÈRE ◎
(START)

**2**

0        1        2
└──┴──┴──┴──┘
    km

SERVOZ ○

MONTVAUTHIER ○

↗N↗

PLAN DE LA CRY ■

▲ L'AIGUILLETTE
  DES HOUCHES

MERLET ■

○ LES BOSSONS

**WALK 10**

are views left to the Aiguille des Grands Montets, with its cable-car and skirts of glaciers culminating in Aiguille Verte.

The path intersection above La Joux hamlet is the first of many on this route: up right leads to La Flégère. Beyond tennis courts at La Chauffria, the path crosses steep scree and rapid progress here will minimise the risk of encountering stonefalls! Road, river and railway are pinched together between Le Lavancher and the inhospitably steep mountainside of La Corruaz along which our route proceeds,

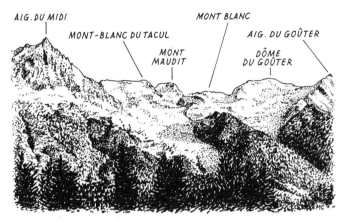

AIG. DU MIDI
MONT-BLANC DU TACUL
MONT BLANC
AIG. DU GOÛTER
MONT MAUDIT
DÔME DU GOÛTER

*View south-east from the Petit Balcon Sud near Chamonix*

once more in forest to **Les Tines'** bridge, adjacent to the railway viaduct.

Follow the 'Chemin du Paradis' alongside the River Arve for approximately 500m and at the next bridge (Pont de la Forge) fork up right (west-south-west) on the lower of two paths. This climbs steadily in bushy forest under the Raffort cliffs and passes beneath **La Flégère** cable-car and out across the broad Couloir des Lanchers (the zig-zag path up right leads to the cable-car station 700m – 2300ft – above).

Emerging only to cross two more couloirs draining Montagne de Charlanon, the Petit Balcon Sud now contours south-west in delightful forest, and where there is open ground the way is embroidered with wonderful wild flowers during June and July.

A jeep-track is reached – keep ahead, ignoring paths up right to La Floria and Charlanon, and another (the jeep-track) down left to Chamonix. (The town centre is only ½ hour distant on foot). Once over Les Nants couloir, the balcon path meanders along from one forest clearing to the next, eventually passing under the **Planpraz** telecabin cable and joining the downhill progress of the Planpraz path for about 150m before forking off right on the level.

**Combe du Brévent** sweeps up dramatically to Le Brévent's imposing summit and a much-used path zig-zags up it to Planpraz. Our itinerary however continues on a much easier option, still well below the main treeline. Leave the Bellachat Refuge path to the right and proceed on the level above the lakes and cliffs of Les Gaillands on the **'Sentier Henri-Vallot'**, dedicated to the memory of Mont Blanc's map-maker. Cross the Couloir des Gaillands, whereafter patchy forest brings you out to the Vouillouds torrent (path down left to Les Bossons).

The onward route twists and turns rather more, and just beyond the Lapaz torrent arrives at **Merlet Mountain Zoo**. From the access road's final bend, turn up right, alongside the perimeter fence, following it round left (south-west) and ignoring first the path to Bellachat Refuge then the one to Chalets de Chailloux, both to the right. Continue down zig-zags but fork off right (west) onto flat ground in forest. The Petit Balcon Sud now passes below the tiny Lac Noir and reaches chalets at **Plan de la Cry**.

This immediate area is criss-crossed by paths, so take care not to go astray! Drop to the left (south-west) on the path to La Flatière for approximately 400m, passing another small lake. Turn right towards Samoteux hamlet and at a junction in about 400m, keep up left in the direction of the houses. This leads on north-west in a gradual descent to **Montvauthier**, being joined half-way along by a path rising from Les Houches via the Chalet Morand.

From Montvauthier, most of the road hairpin bends are short-cut by a direct path, a continuation of which zig-zags down to the Diosaz River not far from a bridge to **Servoz**. A mere 500m to the north-east lie the Diosaz Gorges, well worth a look if time and circumstances permit. (See 'suggested Shorter Walks' at the end of this Chapter).

**Walk 11    Montroc to Les Houches: The Grand Balcon Sud and Le Brévent**

Routing: Montroc – Chalet des Chéserys – La Flégère – Planpraz –
Le Brévent – Bellachat Refuge – Merlet – Les Houches
(Note: This route can be divided up into shorter lengths by descending to the valley from any of several convenient points).

Total ascent: 1302m (4272ft)

Timings: Montroc to Chalet des Chéserys – 3½ hours
Chalet des Chéserys to La Flégère – 1¼ hours
La Flégère to Planpraz – 1¾ hours
Planpraz to Le Brévent – 2 hours
Le Brévent to Bellachat Refuge – ¾ hour
Bellachat Refuge to Les Houches – 1½ hours

Meals, snacks and drinks available at La Flégère, Planpraz, Le Brévent summit (when cable-car is reinstated) and Bellachat Refuge.

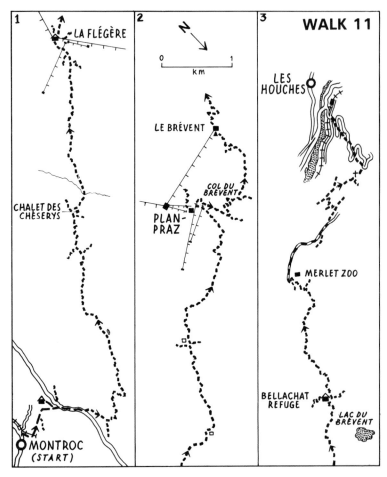

Accommodation at La Flégère and Bellachat.
*Special note: An early start is strongly recommended, as is attempting the walk in reasonably fine weather (although there are numerous escape routes by which to cut the walk short if necessary). Early in the summer there will be snow to cross in places, and even during August it is not uncommon to find extensive snowbanks between Planpraz and*

*Le Brévent summit. Whilst not essential in late season, an ice-axe will be useful on this stretch. Every kind of terrain is encountered, including some exposed sections of path here and there, though gradients are moderate for much of the way.*

This end-to-end traverse of the Aiguilles Rouges massif on the Grand Balcon Sud trail is perhaps the showpiece walk for views of Mont Blanc and the Chamonix Aiguilles; since it is also the route taken by the long-distance Tour du Mont Blanc, it is well waymarked. As progress is made towards the south-west, there is a constant, subtly-shifting panorama across to the high snows and you will be well acquainted with Western Europe's loftiest summit by the end of the day. Not that mountainsides nearer at hand lack interest or variety – there is everything from forest to scree, snowfields to rock scrambling, grassy levels to steep zig-zag paths, as well as fascinating vistas up to the peaks of the Aiguilles Rouges themselves.

There can be no question about the expedition's quality, nor its length, which will test the fittest: over 10 hours of actual walking along with 1300m of ascent demand willing muscles and stamina. In some ways, the route is a synthesis of all others in the Chamonix valley. Coalescing the best of the views and the greatest range of terrain, it encompases in one enormous bite all the individual flavours which make up the experience of walking in this exhilarating area.

Leaving from Montroc, a satellite resort 2km north of Argentière, maximises a walker's chances of returning to the start after reaching Les Houches at the end of a very long day. Bus and train links in the valley are generally good, although obtaining timetables beforehand will take the guesswork from this particular problem.

Walk a little way up the road from **Montroc** railway station (nearby hotel, car parking space) and turn left. In approximately 200m, the path for Tré-le-Champ bends left (south-west) where the railway enters the Montroc Tunnel. Passing houses and over meadowland, the way veers right and rises to the N506 Col des Montets road beyond the Gîte d'étape at **Tré-le-Champ**.

Turn right up the road and in about 500m pass a sign to the right for Les Posettes. Almost immediately turn left into the Aiguilles Rouges Nature Reserve on a variant of the Tour du Mont Blanc routing. The path climbs towards cliffs and is soon joined from the right by another from Col des Montets (an alternative start to this walk), at which point you turn left (west).

A stiff climb lies ahead on numerous zig-zags and round rocky

*Le Brévent cable-car, Mont Blanc in the background*

outcrops towards the as yet unseen 'balcon' above. The roofs of Tré-le-Champ slowly recede below, while across the Arve the northernmost aiguilles shine high and aloof. Once at a rugged shoulder of land at around 2000m (6500ft) – La Remuaz – the **Grand Balcon Sud** proper begins, undulating along past a small, unnamed lake below great, greenish slabs rising in tiers on your right to the rock summit of Aiguille Martin. Around each successive corner, Mont Blanc seems to grow in magnificence, its snow dome buttressed by lesser tops and the undisputed focus of attention.

The rugged path continues in a south-westerly direction and shortly after a fork right to Lac Blanc via the Chéserys lakes (see Walk 14), an intersection is reached at a large, waymarked cairn. Coming up from the left is the main Tour du Mont Blanc path with its famous 'passage délicat' on the Aiguillette d'Argentière. We now join it on the way forward towards La Flégère, clearly visible ahead but still over an hour's tramp away.

Dropping to the **Chalet des Chéserys** (1998m – 6555ft), keep right (west) past the building itself (ignoring the path left which descends to Argentière – a possible escape route). The stony path crosses several small streams draining from Lac Blanc above and only an exposed corner interrupts the easy contouring walk along Montagne

90

de la Flégère. Beyond La Chavanne at the approaches to the cable-car station, you pass under ski-lifts on bare slopes to arrive at the first place of refreshment so far – **La Flégère** (1877m – 6158ft; Refuge privately owned; 100 places; guardian from June to Sept., closed in winter.) Meals, snacks and drinks in the cable-car station bar/restaurant and in the separate refreshment hut. There is a viewing table and a cabin-lift ascends to l'Index (see Walk 14).

From La Flégère, a cable-car descends to Les Praz de Chamonix, as does a pleasant path (Walk 13). Should circumstances dictate, the valley is thus easily reached; allow 1¾ hours by foot. In fine weather you can sit on the terrace and watch paragliders, or with the aid of field glasses the almost imperceptibly small figures of climbers on the snows of Mont Blanc. Other prominent features include the Mer de Glace, the Drus and Aiguille Verte, with the Argentière and Chardonnet aiguilles farther left.

The onward route now descends a flight of steps and turns right (west) towards Planpraz, at first through the upper edge of forest then out across pasture and rough hillside. It is a well walked stage of less than two hours between cable-car stations, and can be accomplished by walkers of most ages and abilities. The ruined chalets of La Glière and Charlanon are passed, and from the latter another escape route descends to the valley.

**Planpraz**, more than La Flégère, has suffered beneath the onslaught of the bulldozer and the amenity developers. Adjacent slopes are very popular with winter skiers, for whose convenience an expanding network of lifts, access tracks and pistes has been established. Without a cosmetic covering of snow, it is not a pretty sight in summer! Add to this a continuous influx of trippers riding up from Chamonix in the cabin-lift, and the modernisation of the Brévent cable-car system involving construction work and disruption to that ride, and it is hardly surprising that Planpraz seems a little the worse for wear. However, the refurbished 'Altitude 2000' bar/restaurant may make amends and, once again, the descending cabin-lift and a good path (2 hours) offer ready-made short-cuts down to Chamonix if required. (The lift closes at 5pm; 6pm July/August).

After almost 7 hours already on the trail, loins may need to be girded up for the next leg – an ascent of Le Brévent, highlight of the whole itinerary and key to a continuation of the route which would otherwise be stalled on the precipitous mountainsides to the north-west of Chamonix.

With just over 4 hours' rugged walking still to do, it would be prudent to take stock before leaving Planpraz. If the weather is deteriorating, the hour getting late or fatigue already taking its toll, it may be advisable to call it a day and enjoy this sensational final stage on another occasion. (At the time of writing, the Brévent cable-car has been out of service for two seasons, but when reinstated would provide another escape route to the valley, at least until around 5pm when it closes).

Still on the Tour du Mont Blanc routing, the path to Col du Brévent veers up left (north-west) from the 'Altitude 2000' bar/restaurant towards ski-lift pylons. Pass a fenced ski piste left and climb right, across steep mountainside, grassy in fact but often snow covered, when an ice-axe is useful. (Under deep snow early in the season, this section needs extra care). About half-way up, a path junction is reached (right leads to the Clocher de Planpraz climbing school crags), at which we swing left (south-west) and rise in zig-zags over probable snowbanks to **Col du Brévent** (2368m – 7769ft).

There are marvellous views from here, not just to Mont Blanc but west to the deep Diosaz valley, Col d'Anterne (Walk 23) and the distant Chablais. From this direction the long-distance GR5 'Grand Traverse of the Alps' joins and is coincident for the remainder of this walk.

More snow and broken rock lead on west-south-west from the col, behind the sharp crest of the Brévent ridge. A rocky scramble or two and eventually stony zig-zags lead up to **Le Brévent** summit (2525m – 8284ft; refreshments, viewing table, cable-car to Planpraz.)

One metre higher than Mont Joly to the south-west (Walk 27), Le Brévent is one of relatively few noteworthy summits attainable by the ordinary mountain walker in this region. First climbed in 1760 by the 20 year old H. B. de Saussure, it is generally considered to be one of the finest viewpoints over Mont Blanc, distinguished from others by its height and its position directly above Chamonix. Indeed, 1500 near-vertical metres (5000ft) to the valley floor are almost as compelling a sight as the glaciers and peaks which rise above it! The Bossons Glacier is especially dramatic, a curving tongue of ice just to the right of the Mont Blanc tunnel portal.

The Brévent 'télépherique' was constructed during 1928-30 and characterises the adventurous civil engineering of that era. The cables span 1348m (4422ft) length and 515m (1690ft) height between their supporting pylons. Until the modernised service is operational, the only visitors to Le Brévent's summit are those who can make it under their own steam; also until then (possibly 1988), there is no short-cut or escape route other than returning to Planpraz or continuing ahead.

A broad, well-maintained but rough path descends in zig-zags south-south-west then follows the ridge's snow-patched, bouldery undulations, with good views over the beautiful Brévent lake to the right. Arriving at a signed path junction, turn left down to the **Bellachat Refuge**, rebuilt in 1981 (2151m – 7057ft; privately owned; 30 places; guardian from end-June to end-Sept. Reservations tel: (50) 53. 43. 23. Meals, snacks and drinks.)

Here begins in earnest the final long descent to the valley (there is a direct path to Chamonix via Plan Lacha – 2½ hours – off left) as the way ahead loses altitude rapidly down many dusty zig-zags and little rocky steps across the precipitous flanks of Aiguillette du Brévent. In the process you cross the Vouillouds ravine, a steep scramble aided with metal rails, but for the most part you are in and out of conifer forest, round exposed little corners above incredible dizzy views.

When the buildings of Merlet wild-life park are visible not far below, turn left (shortly after crossing the Ravin de Lapaz), to emerge alongside the perimeter fence and drop left to the access road near the entrance. **Merlet Mountain Zoo** (1562m – 5125ft) contains species such as chamois, bouquetin, lama, marmot and deer in a 'free range' situation. Meals and drinks are available and there is a powerful telescope for public use, but entry to the zoo is not free!

Follow the partly surfaced road down for about 1km and watch for a waymarked path off left. Avalanche damage has changed the path's course hereabouts and it is necessary to follow waymarks carefully to the huge **Statue du Christ-Roi** which stands 17m high and has a chapel in its base. Made from reinforced concrete by the sculptor M. Serraz and dedicated to peace, it was erected in the 1930's following donations by local residents and holidaymakers.

Continue ahead to the road at chalets and turn down left. After a few initial bends, paths short-cut all the big dog-legs right down to the valley. In all probability, your arrival here will be a rude awakening from the peace of the mountain trail and the easy sound of your own footfall. For at this lower exit from the Chamonix valley, road, railway and river are squeezed together, with major roadbuilding adding to the cacophony and fumes! **Les Houches** and the Chamonix bus-stop unfortunately lie across the busy N205, although the railway station is close by on the right.

**Suggested shorter walks in the Argentière area**

AIGUILLETTE D'ARGENTIÈRE
Total ascent: 483m (1585ft) – 3 hours' walking

Tré-le-Champ hamlet lies just off the N506 road 1km south of Col des Montets. The first section of this walk follows the Tour du Mont Blanc routing so is clearly waymarked and starts just downhill from three chalets on the main road. The 'balcon' path heads up south-west and out over a flatter area – Plan de la Grange. At a path junction, turn up right, still on the TMB, under crags used by a rock-climbing school.

Because of its unique position, this stretch of mountainside offers outstanding views. A short way beyond the Aiguillette d'Argentière is a 'passage délicat' over exposed slabs, aided by metal cable in places, but this itinerary goes no further west. After enjoying this delightful spot, return to the path junction and fork right, down past the Bechar cross. Ignore the first turning left, taking the second instead and drop gradually through forest past the line of an old ski-lift. The main road is reached some 600m below the start, and almost directly opposite a lane leads into lower Tré-le-Champ.

LE TOUR FROM ARGENTIÈRE
Total ascent: 203 (666ft) – 2½ hours' walking

This low-level but interesting walk begins behind Argentière's church on the Chemin du Vieux-Four which climbs gently over meadow past chalets. Turn off right after 300m, passing under the railway line and rising in a series of zig-zags through woods to Le Planet. Keep left (north-east) on the road for approximately 150m and turn off right on the Chemin des Travarchires. There ensues a pleasant descent through forest not far above the village of Montroc. The way forward follows the Bisme torrent (issuing from Le Tour Glacier) up to a footbridge, crosses it and turns left (north-west) on Chemin du Rocher Nay into Le Tour (for details of Le Tour see Walk 7).

On the return, take the middle path from the footbridge – the Petit Balcon Nord – which takes a slightly higher line back towards Le Planet, with comprehensive views right up the Chamonix valley. Keep straight ahead (south) at a path junction, dropping through forest on zig-zags and veering right at the botton to join the Chemin de la Moraine under the railway line and back to Argentière village centre.

## LA PIERRE À BOSSON
Total ascent: 420m (1378ft) – 2¼ hours' walking

Take the Chemin de la Moraine east from Argentière village centre and walk under the railway line. At a path junction, go up left on the Petit Balcon Nord in forest, two large bends leading to a junction. Turn right here (south-east) on a gradually ascending line, crossing several shallow gullies and the deeper Couloir du Rocheray. You are opposite a distinctive spine of moraine and climb sharply to meet its top, shortly after reaching the highest point on this walk adjacent to the Argentière Glacier - La Pierre à Bosson (1670m – 5479ft). It is possible to continue east for 500m on a very rough path (care needed) along the steep flanks of Le Rocheray to the Quaiset stream ravine. The return can be varied by walking through Le Planet and taking the path left off the first road bend.

*Marmot*

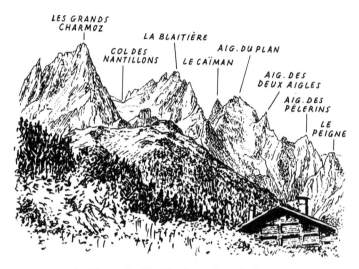

*The Chamonix Aiguilles from above Le Lavancher*

# 3:
# The Chamonix Valley

*Aiguille du Midi from the Chamonix Valley*

**Walk 12    Chalets de la Pendant and the Petit Balcon Nord**

Routing: Le Lavancher – Chalets de la Pendant – Plan Joran – (optional extension to La Croix de Lognan and the Argentière Glacier) – Les Chosalets – Petit Balcon Nord – Le Lavancher. (Les Chosalets can be descended to by cable-car from La Croix de Lognan – end of June to beginning of Sept.)

Total ascent: 668m (2192ft)

Timings: Le Lavancher to Chalets de la Pendant – 1½ hours
La Pendant to Plan Joran – ¾ hour
(Extension to the Argentière Glacier – there and back 2 hours)
Plan Joran to Le Lavancher via the Petit Balcon Nord – 2¼ hours

Meals, snacks and drinks available at Le Lavancher, possibly at new ski development at Plan Joran, and at La Croix de Lognan.

A good deal of this walk threads in and out of forest, making it eminently suitable for an 'easy' day or when the weather seems unpromising, though it is an enjoyable walk in fine conditions too. There is an opportunity to extend the route to take in the Argentière Glacier (see Walk 9 for more detail) and to use the cable-car from the Croix de Lognan intermediate station either to descend to the valley or to ride up to the Aiguille des Grands Montets, a marvellous, glacier-encircled viewpoint above this northern end of the Chamonix valley.

Paths throughout are excellent and take you past a typical alpine farmstead at Chalets de la Pendant, huddled beneath rugged mountainside. The Petit Balcon Nord between Argentière and Les Bois was constructed as recently as 1973 and runs entertainingly along about 200m (650ft) above the valley floor on a ledge of steep wooded hillside.

**Le Lavancher** is a pretty village midway between Chamonix and Argentière. There is parking space at the top (south) of the village, and farther up at the end of the track zig-zags. The walk starts on a good track – Chemin de Mauvais Pas, waymarked Le Chapeau and Lognan – climbing through forest.

At the first path junction turn up left, and at the next junction (waymarked Le Pendant 1 hour 20min, Lognan 2 hours 50min) ignore the path on the left and continue climbing through deep pine forest, now on the **Grand Balcon Nord.** You pass snow retaining walls and eventually, after numerous upward zig-zags, walk out into a bowl

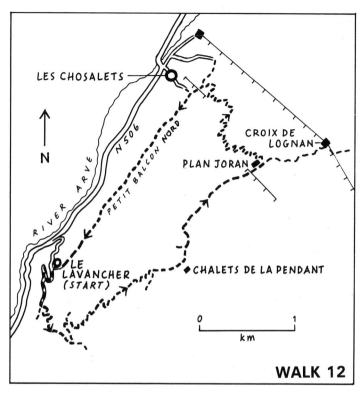

**WALK 12**

of pasture, at the back of which nestle the big low barns and herd of cows at **Chalets de la Pendant** (1778m – 5833ft).

Cutting north-east across this picturesque alp, the path rises gently to meet a broad track at a bend above a ski-lift station (not shown on maps). Turn right, following the track up under a chair-lift. After undulating delightfully along for a while, it rises through larch woods to yet another chair-lift, just beyond which will be seen the large new **Plan Joran** restaurant complex. Geared up for the winter skiing trade, this impressive timber building and terrace does not yet appear on maps. There are good views west across to the great snow-streaked walls of the Aiguilles Rouges.

(Here begins the optional extension to the Croix de Lognan cable-car intermediate station and beyond to the Argentière Glacier.

*Argentière and Col des Montets (centre top) from the path to Plan Joran*

To reach them simply stay on the broad, motorable, track which contours east round the mountainside ahead. Its continuation from the cable-car station leads on, climbing gradually to a waymarked boulder directly above the Chalet Militaire de Lognan by a pylon. Turn up right on a rough path until the edge of the glacier is reached. For more detail please turn to Walk 9. Allow 2 hours for the return walk to the glacier.)

From Plan Joran, this itinerary turns down left on a path generously waymarked with red paint flashes. (Until the ski development is consolidated in this area, there may be minor changes here). The path zig-zags down, always beautifully graded, through mixed woodland with superb views from occasional clearings over Argentière and Col des Montets.

Passing a left fork to La Pendant, continue down the main path and the final steeper zig-zags, to emerge on the **Petit Balcon Nord.** Turn left and at the bottom of the slope pass the path right to nearby Les Chosalets and the Glacier d'Argentière campsite. The balcon path first rises, crosses a torrent bed, then undulates pleasantly along through woods, well above the busy valley floor. In places, the path has been laboriously cut into slopes otherwise far too steep to negotiate.

After about 1½km of delightful progress, the way descends gently and becomes a broad field track, arriving at **Le Lavancher** as the Chemin de Crozat. Le Lavancher is an unspoilt, archetypical Savoyard village, full of ancient timber chalets with their stockpiles of logs stored against the winter snows. Its peaceful, rural ambience is in total contrast to the frenetic activity of nearby Chamonix.

At the road, turn left, then right past chalets up a narrow short-cut path and across the road again. The track ahead rises to reach the road just left of car parking space. Turn left, walk up past a hotel/bar and left round the final bends to the start.

### Walk 13   La Flégère and Lac Blanc

Routing: Chamonix – La Flégère – Lac Blanc – La Flégère – Descend to Les Praz by cable-car – Chamonix

Total ascent: 1287m (4222ft)

Timings: Chamonix to La Flégère – 2½ hours
La Flégère to Lac Blanc – 1¾ hours
Descent to La Flégère – 1¼ hours
La Flégère to Chamonix using cable car – 1 hours (or 2½ hours by foot)

Meals, snacks, drinks and accommodation available at the Flégère Refuge. Meals, snacks and drinks only at Lac Blanc Refuge.

*Special note: Early in the season and possibly well into August if winter snowfall has been heavy or late, the upper reaches of the path will be snow covered. Although gradients are generally moderate, some steep passages might need ice-axe safeguarding under such conditions and it is advisable to take precautions against sunburn and glare.*

To reach Lac Blanc is one of the classic outings for walkers in the Chamonix region and unless it is heavily snow covered, there are no difficulties on the trail. For this reason alone, you cannot expect to have it to yourself! Not only is the lake in a truly remarkable setting, facing unsurpassed views of the entire Mont Blanc range, but La Flégère cable-car encourages visitors who would otherwise be deterred by a climb from the valley to make the lesser ascent of some 2 to 3 hours.

In fact, the walk from the valley up to La Flégère is a delight and is incorporated into this route. (For an alternative excursion in this magnificent area starting from La Flégère, see Walk 14). The author recommends using the cable-car to descend to the valley floor only in order to save wear and tear on knees and feet! However, to walk the whole way up and down would make a satisfying and commendable

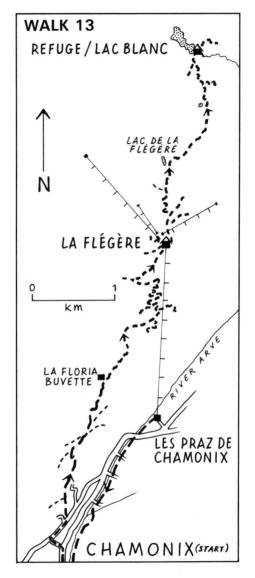

**WALK 13**

REFUGE / LAC BLANC

N

LAC DE LA FLÉGÈRE

LA FLÉGÈRE

0    1
km

LA FLORIA
BUVETTE

RIVER ARVE

LES PRAZ DE
CHAMONIX

CHAMONIX (START)

expedition for the purists among us!

On the west side of the River Arve, walk north from **Chamonix** town centre and turn left before the hospital, then right, along a quiet suburban road at Les Plans. Go left up Chemin de la Floria (also signed La Flégère and Petit Balcon Sud) and turn off right at the first bend onto a broad, stony track going uphill in the vicinity of Les Nants. Pass an electricity sub-station, cross a torrent and in a short while the 'Petit Balcon Sud' path (see Walk 10) forks off right. We continue up the broad track and in some 20min. arrive at the **Chalet la Floria buvette** (1337m – 4386ft; snacks, drinks). For such a relatively low altitude, views of Mont Blanc from this charming, flowery and immaculately kept chalet are impressive.

Now much narrower, the path continues along through forest then contours round the open, grassy Couloir des Lanchers where you'll find a profusion of wild flowers during late June/early July. In a few hundred metres, a path junction is reached, at which fork up left (right leads down to Les Praz). Ignore a turning right to Les Tines underneath the cable-car and after a couple of zig-zags, pass another path off left to des Grandes. Continue on up, twisting and turning, cross over a ski piste and veer left (west) into forest. You double back right onto another stony piste which, unfortunately, has obliterated the original path and has to be followed up less than comfortably but not for long before arriving at the upper limit of La Corrua forest.

Here stands **La Flégère Refuge** (1877m – 6158ft. Privately owned; 100 places; guardian from June to September, closed in winter; reservations tel: (50) 53.06.13. Meals, snacks, drinks in the cable-car station; refreshment bar.) La Flégère is the top station of the cable-car from Les Praz de Chamonix, and bottom station for a telecabin lift up to l'Index (see Walk 14). There is a viewing table, and indeed the spectacle of the Mont Blanc chain, with its Aiguilles, glaciers and high snows, is well worth making the effort to see, walker or non-walker. Even richer rewards await those who can continue to Lac Blanc. . . .

Walk up to the right of the cable-car station where you will find a sign 'Lac Blanc 1hr.45min'. Go down the rough track (north) beneath La Trappe chair-lift, then turn left (waymarked) past La Chavanne chalet (an ancient sheepfold now owned by the French army's mountaineering school) and on up stony zig-zags. Fork right off the bulldozed track on a path towards a chalet building ahead. (Note: there is always the risk of route changes hereabouts as new ski development takes place. If snow conceals stretches of the trail, it is

*Lac Blanc Refuge. Mont Blanc top right*

waymarked with occasional paint flashes on rocks.)

The path meanders up in a northerly direction, past **Lac de la Flégère** on the left and past a large cairn, where it enters the Aiguilles Rouges Nature Reserve. The clear track contouring along 150m (500ft) below is the 'Grand Balcon Sud', used by the long-distance Tour du Mont Blanc trail.

The way ascends steadily over mixed terrain, passes a tiny lake left (often frozen over till mid-summer), then rises more steeply in a series of rocky steps and zig-zag bends. A path connecting with the Chalet des Chéserys (see Walk 14) joins from the right (east), whereafter you are increasingly likely to be climbing over snow, at least until mid-July.

Beyond a waymarking signpost where the Index traverse comes in from the left (south-west) – see Walk 14 – it only remains to mount a curving lip of ground and there before you is the lake and **Lac Blanc Refuge** (2352m – 7716ft; privately owned; open June to September, depending on snow conditions. Meals, snacks and drinks.)

*Early season walkers on a snowed-over Lac Blanc. Col du Belvedère top centre*

For walkers holding an image in mind from postcards and tourist literature, the refuge may be something of a disappointment, at least until some funds are available! A recent avalanche completely destroyed its upper storey, so that it has lost its attractive gable ends and the ability to offer accommodation. Also, the delectable sight of the Mont Blanc massif reflected in Lac Blanc's tranquil waters is a fairly elusive one, demanding still air and freedom from surface snow and ice. Best chances are in September!

Beyond a narrow neck, the lake opens out, and farther still a vast bowl of mountainside swells to the Aiguille du Belvédère and other climbs in the Aiguilles Rouges accessible from here. To the east, a path leaves for the 5 diminutive Chéserys lakes (see Walk 14), but unless this extension is to be added to today's itinerary, return to La Flégère by the ascent route.

Take the cable-car down to **Les Praz** (last departure 5.30pm July and August, 5pm June and September) and walk from the bottom station along the south bank of the River Arve for about 500m. Cross the road just before a left bend and continue ahead on a shady riverside promenade, past tennis courts, campsite and the modern sports centre, all the way into Chamonix.

### Walk 14   L'Index, Lac Blanc and the Chéserys Lakes

Routing:   La Flégère – l'Index – Lac Blanc – Lacs des Chéserys – Chalet des Chéserys – La Flégère. (The route assumes that the cable-car is taken up to the start at La Flégère. If time is short, the telecabin lift can be taken to l'Index, deducting 1¼ hours from the walk.)

Total ascent: 508m (1667ft)

Timings:   La Flégère to l'Index – 1½ hours
         l'Index to Lac Blanc – 1¼ hours
         Lac Blanc to La Flégère via Chéserys lakes – 2¼ hours (or direct – 1¼ hours)

Meals, snacks, drinks and accommodation available at La Flégère Refuge; meals, snacks and drinks only at Lac Blanc Refuge.

*Special note: On the initial climb to l'Index and thereafter on the traverse which maintains height at around 2300m (7500ft) as far as the Chéserys lakes, there are likely to be some snow slopes to cross; early in the season, much of this upper section of trail will be snow covered. In such conditions, walkers are advised to take spare warm clothing, sunhat, suncream and sunglasses, while an ice-axe will provide security on the steeper slopes. Obtain a weather forecast before setting out, since not only is the route exposed for most of its length, but its*

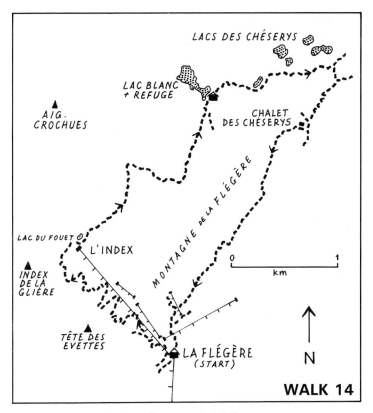

LACS DES CHÉSERYS

LAC BLANC
+ REFUGE

AIG.
CROCHUES

CHALET
DES CHÉSERYS

MONTAGNE DE LA FLÉGÈRE

LAC DU FOUET

L'INDEX

0        1

km

INDEX
DE LA
GLIÈRE

TÊTE DES
EVETTES

LA FLÉGÈRE
(START)

N

**WALK 14**

*great attractiveness depends on good visibility.*

By starting the walk at La Flégère, it is possible to spend longer at altitude and thus considerably extend an exploration of this spectacularly beautiful part of the Aiguilles Rouges. Throughout the upper traverse, you will be in high mountain terrain and enjoying definitive views of the Mont Blanc range. The stretch from l'Index to Lac Blanc is quite rugged in places, but elsewhere the trail is straightforward enough.

With time to spare and in suitable conditions, the shores of both Lac Blanc and the 5 Lacs des Chéserys are worth strolling around. The final hour or so of the walk is spent on the 'Grand Balcon Sud'

*On the traverse from L'Index to Lac Blanc*

which runs along a natural shelf half way up between valley and the Aiguilles Rouges tops, all the way from Col des Montets to above Les Houches. It is used by walkers on the Tour du Mont Blanc long-distance footpath and, in part, by those on the GR5 en route from Lake Geneva to Nice.

Outside the cable-car top station at **La Flégère**, take the signed path to l'Index (north-west), climbing in zig-zags not far from the telecabin lift to a small plateau rich in alpine flora. (Note: ski development might impinge on the path during this ascent routing). Following the general direction of the telecabin, and directly beneath it at times, the path continues to ascend in big zig-zags, with the impressive Tête des Evettes up left.

Ignoring turnings off, you climb steadily, negotiate some small combes and, as height is gained, begin to cross snowbanks (depending on the time of year). Index de la Glière, up to the left, is a popular rock-climbing ground; not far beyond stands the **Index** telecabin top station at 2385m (7825ft). There is summer skiing on these slopes.

Descend to the right (generally north-east) towards and beyond the small, often frozen Lac du Fouet. The way is steep in places, requiring care as it drops over broken mountainside and probable snowbanks into the vast, rugged Combe des Aiguilles Crochues.

Swinging south-east, you come round a rocky shoulder before veering north-east again and climbing more determinedly at the perimeter of the Aiguilles Rouges Nature Reserve.

Another rather exposed stretch is passed, then once again the route forward is over an uneven mixture of stones, rock and snow as you gradually gain height and converge on the path up from La Flégère direct to Lac Blanc (see Walk 13) which is joined at a waymarking signpost. 200m over a rise stands the **Lac Blanc Refuge** (2352m – 7716ft) privately owned; open June to September, depending on snow conditions; Meals, snacks and drinks).

With its upper storey demolished by a recent avalanche, the refuge cannot for the time being offer overnight accommodation. It is nonetheless a very popular destination at the conjunction of several trails from different starting points in the valley. Lac Blanc is notoriously late to thaw out and early in the season may be completely snow covered; however, it is rightly considered to be one of the premier viewpoints over the Mont Blanc massif, which is ranged along the south-east skyline.

The walk continues in a general direction slightly north of east, first rounding a rocky knoll to where the path drops suddenly over very steep slopes to the first of the **Chéserys lakes**. This is one location where an ice-axe will certainly help early in the season, when you may be confronted by an intimidating snow slope, though with care you are unlikely to come to harm.

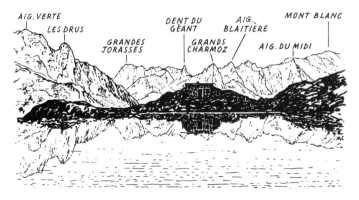

*The Mont Blanc Massif from Lac Blanc*

*On the Grand Balcon Sud, last section of walk 14*

Beyond the first lake, keep to the upper path which rises behind a small hill, descends, then contours for about 500m. Pass 2 paths down right, but turn sharp right at the third to reach a large waymarking cairn and sign at a major junction between the Tour du Mont Blanc and a variant. Keep ahead, then descend more steeply and take the second right turn to the **Chalet des Chéserys** on the Plan d'Aiguilles Rouges. Directly opposite to your left will be the Argentière Glacier and Aiguille du Chardonnet (approached on Walks 9 and 7), and to your right the Dru, Aiguille Verte and Mer de Glace (see Walk 15).

Following Tour du Mont Blanc waymarks (red and white paint flashes), the route now proceeds west, crosses the torrent draining from Lac Blanc, veers south-west and contours along the Montagne de la Flégère towards the increasingly conspicuous cable-car station. A couple of high, rocky corners are rounded before arriving at the erstwhile sheepfold of La Chavanne. Passing beneath La Trappe ski-lift, climb the final stony slopes to La Flégère for the cable-car down. (Final departures – 5pm June/September; 5.30pm July/August.)

**Walk 15   Montenvers to Plan de l'Aiguille: The Grand Balcon Nord**
Routing:  Chamonix – Chalet des Planards – Buvette Caillet – Montenvers/Mer de Glace – Signal Forbes – Grand Balcon

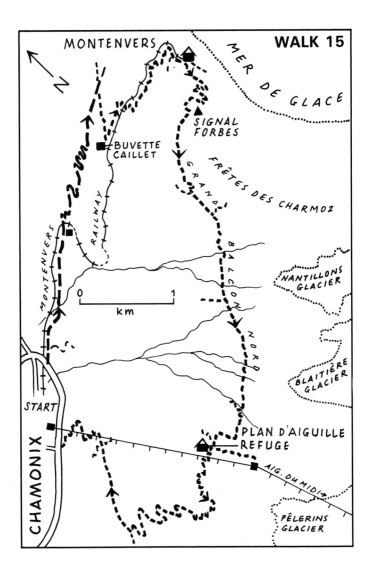

WALK 15

MONTENVERS

MER DE GLACE

N

SIGNAL FORBES

BUVETTE CAILLET

FRÊTES DES CHARMOZ

RAILWAY

GRANDI

NANTILLONS GLACIER

MONTENVERS

BALCON

0          1

km

NORD

BLAITIÈRE GLACIER

START

PLAN D'AIGUILLE REFUGE

CHAMONIX

AIG. DU MIDI

PÉLERINS GLACIER

Nord – Refuge du Plan de l'Aiguille – Chamonix.

Total ascent: 1272m (4173ft)

Timings: Ascent from Chamonix to Montenvers – 2½ hours

Montenvers to Plan de l'Aiguille – 2½ hours

Plan de l'Aiguille to Chamonix – 2 hours

(A rack and pinion railway runs from Chamonix to Montenvers and could be used to shorten the route: deduct 2 hours from the ascent. The final descent from Plan de l'Aiguille to Chamonix can be made by cable-car if required.)

Drinks and snacks available at Buvette Caillet; meals, drinks and accommodation at Hôtel-Refuge Montenvers; meals, drinks and accommodation at Refuge du Plan de l'Aiguille.

*Special note: Early in the season, steep snow banks may cover the trail on the north-facing slopes of the 'balcon' traverse.*

Taken in its entirety, this walk gives a very full and entertaining day on the trail, especially if extra time is given to visiting the museum/zoo at Montenvers and to descending to the Mer de Glace. However, should time, weather or other factors suggest a shortening of the walk itself, there is mechanised transport to and from both ends of the traverse.

The Grand Balcon Nord (another section of which extends north-east to the Argentière glacier, see Walk 9) typifies 'middle mountain' terrain: that is, above the afforested valley sides and high pasture but just below the terminal moraines of glaciers and the screes falling from the precipitous Aiguilles de Chamonix. You really have the best of both worlds – an airy view over Chamonix far below, across to the Brévent and Aiguilles Rouges opposite, and proximity to the grandeur of elemental mountain scenery in the form of soaring rock, scree, snow and ice. Access to either end of the 'balcon' traverse is pleasant and mostly in shady forest. The paths are well maintained and, needless to say, well walked, though much depends upon the time of your visit.

The **Montenvers mountain railway** (Chemin de Fer du Montenvers) will be found adjacent to Chamonix's S.N.C.F. station to the east of the town centre. With the Montenvers railway on your left, cross the main N506 road and walk towards the conspicuous 'Luge d'Été (a summer toboggan run and chair -lift, well worth a ride!). Keep ahead up the broad stony track to the right of the run; it crosses it and continues up by the edge of trees.

POINTE MARGUERITE
POINTE WHYMPER
POINTE WALKER
COL DES
HIRONDELLES
MONT MALLET
DÔME DE
ROCHEFORT

*The Mer de Glace from Montenvers*

The railway track is crossed at **Chalet des Planards** (goats' cheese for sale), whereafter the wide woodland track zig-zags steadily up, with views left over the Chamonix valley growing in interest as height is gained and more of the town and its environs are revealed. Constructed in 1968, the track being followed is known as the 'Sortie de la Vallée Blanche', being utilised in forestry work and by winter skiers returning to the valley.

About 1km (½ mile) after leaving the zig-zags behind, watch for a cross-junction of paths and turn up sharp right, waymarked 'Caillet, Montenvers'. **Buvette Caillet** (snacks/drinks) is soon reached and here turn left, still zig-zagging up through forest. Cross the railway again, turning right and climbing through attractive larch woods to emerge by the railway once more and, a little further on, at the

113

*Mer de Glace from the path to Signal Forbes*

**Montenvers** top station (1913m – 6276ft.). The imposing hôtel-refuge has accommodation for some 120 souls in rooms and dormitories and was much in demand by climbers and mountaineers as a high point of departure for routes in the vicinity. Its popularity, however, was eclipsed by the construction of the Aiguille du Midi cable-car which now delivers alpinists some 1930m (6300ft) higher up, right into the heart of the Mont Blanc massif. The hôtel-refuge is privately owned, open from the beginning of June to the end of September and offers restaurant service as well as serving snacks and drinks.

## About Montenvers

You will be mingling with many tourists who have come up by

mountain railway, but nevertheless may wish to 'see the sights' before moving on to less frequented parts. Indeed, it was two Englishmen – Messrs Windham and Pocock – who in 1741 climbed le Montenvers and whose evocative accounts of the spectacle they beheld subsequently fired the imaginations of many artists, writers and musicians. A 'Temple of Nature' was built in 1798, now the alpine museum, and long before the railway came into service (in 1909), Montenvers was visited by guided mule-trains bearing such noteworthy pilgrims as Goëthe, Shelley, Byron, Liszt, Victor Hugo and Napoleon III.

The visual feast remains undiminished in intensity. Fed by the eternal snows of the Mont Blanc massif, the **Mer de Glace** is a great, twisting river of ice bounded by the Drus and Aiguille Verte to the east, the Grandes-Jorasses to the south-east and the Grands Charmoz ridges to the west. Second only in size in the whole of Europe to Switzerland's Aletsch glacier, Mer de Glace is, however, receding at the rate of 7m a year. Back in the 17th century it extended right down to the Arve valley. As recently in climatological time as 115 years ago, the torrent beneath Mer de Glace excavated a huge cave at the lower extremity of the ice each summer and this became a well known tourists' attraction (the Grotte d'Arveyron).

For a closer, some may say trivialised, encounter, take the cable-car down to the glacier to view the sculpted 'Ice Cave' and the effects of light and water within crevasses. The Mer de Glace 'flows' at a rate of about 1.5m per week and each grey chevron on its surface is formed by debris deposited during summer rockfalls.

Before leaving Montenvers, you may wish to take a look at the nearby alpine zoo. Mountain species such as marmot, chamois and birds of prey are represented, but it is difficult to avoid feeling that to incarcerate them in this way is an unkind denial of their wild nature, made all the more incongruous by this mountain setting.

To continue the walk, leave past the museum on one of several paths in this eminently accessible and delectable spot, eventually keeping south on a well-made path parallel to the Mer de Glace. If anything, the situation confronting walkers here, amidst superlative alpine scenery, grows even more stunning. It may be possible to spot tiny figures on the glacier far below.

The path soon begins to zig-zag up over rocky slopes, arriving in about 40 mins. at **Signal Forbes** (named after the 19th century Scottish geologist James Forbes), a magnificent viewpoint on the northern spur of the Frêtes des Charmoz at 2198m (7211ft). The retrospective view to Aiguille Verte is immensely impressive. Keeping ahead in the same direction, the way descends at first gently then in a series of zig-zags before levelling off and maintaining height at around 2100m (6890ft).

Undulating along on this natural shelf – **the Grand Balcon Nord** – one is held between high snows and glaciers and the deep Chamonix valley, beyond which rise the south-facing walls of the Brévent and Aiguilles Rouges.

Pass a path right (Chamonix via the Blaitière chalets and a possible short-cut) and continue ahead over torrent beds and snow patches to the edge of a broad basin – the Plan de l'Aiguille. Rising a little, the path rounds a corner to the small **Plan de l'Aiguille Refuge** (2233m – 7326ft. Privately owned; 60 places; open from the beginning of June; meals and drinks. Reservations contact Mr. C. Tournier, La Frasse, Chamonix.)

A short distance up to the left (south) stands the intermediate station of the Aiguille du Midi cable-car which could be used to descend to the valley. The walk down however, though lengthy, is on well graded paths with good views and in pleasant forest lower down.

There are near vertical glimpses of Chamonix 1200m (4000ft) below as the stony path goes beneath the cable-car and begins its winding descent to the valley floor. In good visibility it is possible to make out the 'normal' route up Mont Blanc, a wide trail stamped in the distant snow to the left of the Dôme de Goûter.

Zig-zags are many, but the more there are the easier the gradient and a steady pace will be welcomed by knees and feet! After a considerable loss of altitude (about 800m – 2600ft) and now in forest, a path junction is reached. (The Cascade du Dard is 30min. away left, the Mont Blanc Tunnel 40min., and Les Pelerins, a good route for the west and south of Chamonix, 50min.) This walk continues down right, straight ahead at the next junction (to Les Molliasses) and on down through lovely wild flowers and the heady scent of pine forest. A steeper stretch leads past a ski jump building and out to the large car park serving the Aiguille du Midi Télépherique. An underpass permits safe access to Chamonix beneath the busy N506.

### Walk 16  The Cornu and Noirs Lakes

Routing: Planpraz – Col du Lac Cornu – a) Lac Cornu – b) Col de la
        Glière – Les Lacs Noirs. Return by same routes.
Total ascent: a) 415m (1362ft)
          b) 536m (1758ft)
Timings: a) Ascent – 2 hours. Descent – 1¼ hours

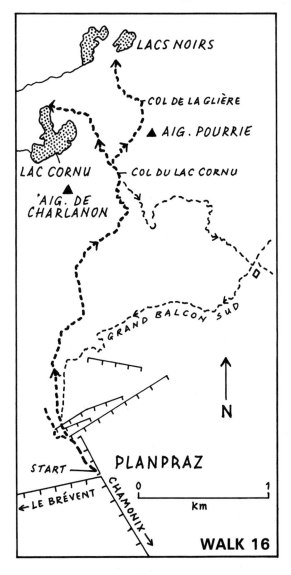

LACS NOIRS

COL DE LA GLIÈRE

▲ AIG. POURRIE

LAC CORNU

COL DU LAC CORNU

▲ AIG. DE CHARLANON

GRAND BALCON SUD

N

PLANPRAZ

START

0        km        1

← LE BRÉVENT

CHAMONIX

WALK 16

b) Ascent – 2 hours. Descent – 1¼ hours

Meals, snacks and drinks available at the Altitude 2000 bar/restaurant on Planpraz.

*Special note: Early in the season and sometimes well into August, snow will cover parts of the trail, especially its upper reaches. On the whole, gradients are not dangerously steep, but in such conditions an ice-axe will prove extremely useful both as a steadying 'third leg' on narrow, slippery trods along snowslopes, and to arrest a possible slip. Good visibility and reasonable weather are needed to enjoy these high locations to the full, so obtain a forecast before setting out. In addition to the usual gear, spare warm clothing, good sunglasses or snow goggles, suncream and a hat will cover most eventualities, especially if going up in sunny and snowy conditions.*

Neither of these expeditions is long and it is quite feasible to combine them, since they share a common routing for three-quarters of the ascent. It is equally feasible to walk up to Planpraz from Chamonix on the Combe du Brévent path (allow 3 hours). However, by taking the cabin-lift, more time is left for walking at higher altitude and this itinerary is certainly not one to hurry.

The Cornu and Noirs lakes are popular destinations for walkers and attract the more intrepid day-trippers from the cabin-lift ride too, although not all of them make it the whole way! Planpraz can seem a busy place. At the time of writing, the Brévent cable-car is being refurbished and the service has been suspended for the past two seasons while construction workers improve the intermediate and top stations. Meanwhile, the cabin-lift ferries sightseers from the valley up 1000m of altitude to visit the recently modernised bar/restaurant and to watch paragliders launching themselves into space and soaring over Chamonix.

Once the strollers around Planpraz have been left behind, this walk takes on a wilder countenance as it climbs into the heart of the Aiguilles Rouges over Col du Lac Cornu and Col de la Glière. The lakes themselves are of unusual shape, though they can remain frozen and partly obscured by snow for much of the summer. It is easier on the descent than on the ascent to take in the majestic sight of the Chamonix Aiguilles and Mont Blanc rising to the south-east across the deep trench of the Arve valley – a classic view of the massif and one shared with other routes on this flank of the Aiguilles Rouges.

The cabin-lift leaves **Chamonix** from the top of La Mollard, a road

*On the trail to the Cornu and Noirs lakes. The distant Aiguille du Tour centre right*

leading up from the Office du Tourisme in the town centre. (During the summer, the lift runs from 8.45am to 5pm; in July and August from 7.30am to 6pm).

From the top station at **Planpraz** walk up past the Altitude 2000 bar/restaurant. A little farther up is a flatter, stony area where two routes diverge: up to the left lies Col du Brévent and the Brévent summit (see Walk 11), while down to the right under a ski-lift is the Tour du Mont Blanc trail which is followed for about 100m. Here you fork off left on the upper path to Lac Cornu over grassy slopes.

The extent and disposition of snowbanks will influence progress, but where the trail is uncovered it is well constructed as it climbs gradually across rugged mountainside falling from the Aiguille de Charlanon. The often stony path, with zig-zags and rocky steps, crosses a huge fan of coarse scree to a narrow 'brèche' (gap) through rocks. Beyond, more rising traverse across steepish scree, and some stiff zig-zags lead up north to **Col du Lac Cornu** (2414m – 7920ft).

A short distance farther on, **Lac Cornu** (2276m – 7467ft) is in view, reached down a path which, although marked with cairns and paint flashes, is more often than not a snowy trudge needing care in places.

b) To find Les Lacs Noirs it is necessary to retrace your steps almost up to Col du Lac Cornu (from where a descent back to Planpraz can be made using the ascent route). Just before the col, a stony, rather indistinct path at times climbs left (north-east) across the flanks of Aiguille Pourrie to the well signed **Col de la Glière** (2461m – 8074ft). To your right (east), Combe de la Glière falls away impressively towards La Flégère.

Waymarked clearly by a large cairn, the path now rises north-west and veers right (north) up a small valley to emerge just above the upper **Lac Noir** (2535m – 8317ft); the lower lake is situated behind an intervening knoll a little way to the west.

Cradled high in the Aiguilles Rouges massif, these small stretches of water, frequently frozen and surrounded by snow-streaked mountainside, form a wild and savagely beautiful foreground for views of Mont Blanc and the Chamonix Aiguilles. There are few situations accessible to walkers which have a sharper alpine ambience than this one, and if time and weather permit, an hour or two spent exploring in the vicinity will be well rewarded.

To return to Planpraz, simply reverse the upward route, although an alternative exists from Col du Lac Cornu. Just over the col, on the Chamonix side, a path forks left (south-south-east) down the side of the Arête Supérieure de Charlanon, drops acutely left (north) from about half-way down onto the extensive slopes of Montagne de

Charlanon and swings back south-east in numerous tight zig-zags down to the Grand Balcon Sud trail. Turn right (south-west) and follow the well-tramped path (on the Tour du Mont Blanc) back to Planpraz. Allow an extra ½ hour for this alternative descent.

## Walk 17   The Blaitière and Grand Chalets

Routing:  Chamonix – Blaitière-dessous – Le Grand Chalet – Blaitière-dessus – Chamonix

Total ascent: 880m (2887ft)

Timings:  Chamonix to Blaitière-dessous – 2 hours
Blaitière-dessous to Le Grand Chalet – ¾ hour
Le Grand Chalet to Chamonix via Blaitière-dessus – 2½ hours

*Special note: The rough paths linking the Blaitière and Grand chalets are susceptible to early-season snowbanks where they cross the Grépon torrent. Due to the steepness of the ground, care is needed at such times.*

This itinerary explores Montagne de Blaitière, mixed terrain of rocky outcrops, torrent gullies, forest and grassy alps midway between the Grand Balcon Nord and the valley. All three chalets and sheepfolds visited were in farm use for many decades, but Le Grand Chalet – the least accessible – has fallen into ruin. From the walk's upper section there are unusually dramatic views of the Chamonix Aiguilles soaring against the south-eastern skyline.

Facing the summer toboggan run (Luge d'Été) from the **Montenvers mountain railway station** (adjacent to Chamonix's S.N.C.F. station), cross the N506 and walk right, across the car park, to the start of Chemin de la Cascade (the Cascade de Blaitière is a 35min stroll up from here). At a track junction in about 100m, turn left (north-east) off the waterfall route and walk up along the edge of trees to a right bend, after which the path begins climbing in forest on a long series of zig-zags.

Off a left hairpin bend, a path leads right (west) to the Blaitière waterfall, only about 250m distant and a worthwhile little detour. Reaching the Blaitière torrent valley near the top of the forest, the way forks sharp left (north-east) and climbs over open pasture to **Blaitière-dessous** (1708m – 5604ft), overlooking the Chamonix valley and the flanks of the Brévent, with the Planpraz cabin-lift clearly visible.

Turn left (east) behind the main chalet building and follow the

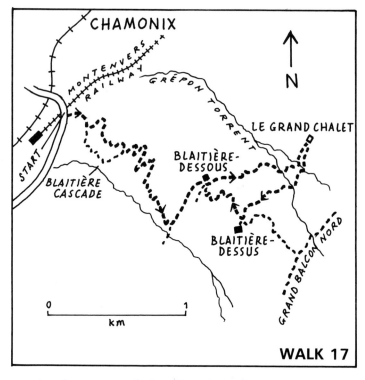

rough path over stream beds and into the larger gully of the Grépon torrent (possible steep snowbanks). A side torrent bed is crossed and an exit made from this sizeable combe up to the ruins of **Le Grand Chalet** (1910m – 6266ft), standing on a grassy shelf backed by rocks. Free from surrounding tree cover, there are exciting views up to the snows and rock peaks of the Chamonix Aiguilles and across to the Aiguilles Rouges massif.

Our onward route now takes the path a little to the east of the upward path, dropping to cross the Grépon torrent some 200m higher up. Once over it, there is not much climbing left to do as the way leads through the upper limit of forest to the more substantial buildings of **Blaitière-dessus** (1926m – 6319ft) at the top of the Blaitière torrent valley.

In fact, the path you have just crossed to reach the chalet connects with the Grand Balcon Nord 200m higher and 750m distant. This opens up variations for the descent, including a cable-car ride down from Plan de l'Aiguille, or a walk down via the Plan de l'Aiguille Refuge; alternatively a ride down in the mountain train from Montenvers, or indeed a walk down via Montenvers. For details of these paths and rides please see Walk 15.

This itinerary's descent takes to the main valley-bound path (north-west) and passes Blaitière-dessous, after which the upward routing is simply reversed.

### Walk 18   Gare des Glaciers

Routing: Mont Blanc Tunnel car park – La Para – Aiguillette de la Tour – Gare des Glaciers. Return by same route.

Total ascent: 1140m (3740ft)

Timings: Tunnel parking to La Para – 1¼ hours
La Para to Gare des Glaciers – 2½ hours
Descent – 2¼ hours

*Special note: There is little respite from climbing on this route, most of which follows zig-zags over steep ground: a good level of fitness is therefore required for maximum enjoyment. So great is the risk of avalanche from the Pélerins Glacier and Aiguille du Midi that a sector of mountainside below them (including the upper part of this route) is closed for access between 1st November and 30th May each year. Walkers intending to visit this area very early in the season are advised to enquire as to its safety before setting out. In any case, snow is likely to be encountered on the higher stretches of this walk well into the summer, and in such conditions an ice-axe, sunglasses or goggles and suncream will be useful additions to normal gear. Due to the absence of refreshment points en route, energy rations will need to be carried up too. Obtaining a weather forecast is recommended as the route is consistently exposed above La Para.*

For most of its length, this walk follows up the line of the original Aiguille du Midi cable-car – the 'Funiculaire Aérien' – the first of its kind in the world and a concept which dates back to the beginning of this century. Work began in 1911 but the project was interrupted by World War I and the final section from Gare des Glaciers to the Aiguille du Midi was never completed. A new and even more audacious line, adopted by the Italian engineer Dino Lora Totino, finally proved successful and remains so to this day.

For some considerable time, the path was the recognised first stage on the ascent of Mont Blanc, but it is better known now for its use by

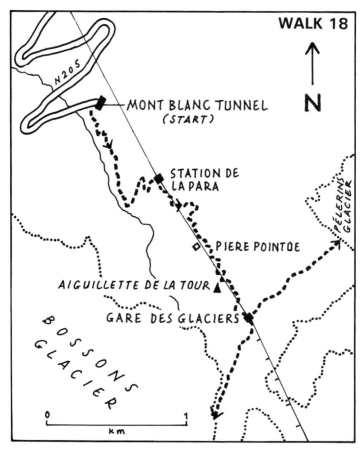

**WALK 18**

↑
**N**

MONT BLANC TUNNEL
*(START)*

STATION DE
LA PARA

◇ PIERE POINTOE

AIGUILLETTE DE LA TOUR ▲

GARE DES GLACIERS

B O S S O N S
G L A C I E R

PÉLERINS GLACIER

N205

0                    1
**k m**

competitors bent on setting ever faster records for the ascent from Chamonix to Mont Blanc and back: the present best time stands at around 8 hours!

Six rather tortuous kilometres from Chamonix up the busy N205 bring you to the **Mont Blanc Tunnel** portal, before which is a large car parking area on the right (1271m – 4170ft). Walk back 150m or so, passing behind avalanche protection, and find the start of a path threading up south in forest alongside the Creuse torrent ravine. The zig-zags begin almost immediately and rapidly become a feature of the walk! Admittedly there is a more level section for some 300m following a left bend (north-east), but further twisting ascent leads up to **Station de la Para** – first stage of the old 'téléphérique' (1685m – 5528ft).

Tree cover is left behind as the serpentine path mounts steep and rugged slopes, south-east towards the ruins of **Piere Pointue** (2038m – 6686ft). With luck and patience, it is sometimes possible to spot chamois hereabouts – an elusive creature in this region so frequented by man. Ever steeper mountainside ensues and the path is forced into tight zig-zags, each stacked above the others; rewards for your toil, however, are entry into an increasingly wild high-mountain environment and dizzy views back down to the valley.

Although of only academic interest to walkers, the Mont Blanc Tunnel lies almost 1000 vertical metres (3300ft) directly below your feet, deep in the heart of the massif on its 11.6km course towards Courmayeur in Italy. Beneath the Aiguille du Midi, the tunnel's 'roof' is 2480m (8136ft) thick. Boring began in December 1958 in Italy and 6 months later in France, the two sides meeting on August 14th 1962. The tunnel was officially opened in 1965 and remained the longest in the world until 1978. Its construction cost the lives of 23 men.

Beyond **Aiguillette de la Tour**, snowbanks may be encountered, especially early in the summer, and as the **Gare des Glaciers** is approached you become more acutely aware of the frozen weight of ice and rock suspended above you. To the east is the Pélerins Glacier, to the west the fabulous Bossons Glacier, but dominating all are the beetling ridges and precipices of Aiguille du Midi, its scale established by the tiny cable-cars inching their way to the summit at 3800m (12,467ft).

From the old cable-car station, a service cableway runs up to Refuge des Cosmiques (3600m – 11,811ft). There is a viewing table here at 2414m (7920ft), the highest point of this itinerary. It is perfectly feasible, however, to continue south-west to the very edge of the **Bossons Glacier** on a rather precarious path, or to descend north-east, again largely over moraine, to the edge of the **Pélerins Glacier**. (The latter can be crossed for a cable-car descent from Plan de l'Aiguille, but should only be attempted by those with the necessary experience and hardware.)

In fine weather conditions, this is a spot to linger in, for as well as your memorably impressive immediate surroundings, prospects to the north take in the entire Aiguilles Rouges range, from Le Brévent

*Gare des Glaciers, the Bossons Glacier (centre) and
Mont Blanc from Le Brévent*

just across the valley, to Aiguille du Belevédère and beyond. If
rushed, knees and feet will take a hammering on the descent: in any
case, facing away from the slope without the exertions of the ascent
allows for a more leisurely appreciation of the outstanding scenery.

### Walk 19   Montagne de la Côte and La Jonction
Routing: Le Mont – Chalet du Glacier des Bossons – Chalet des

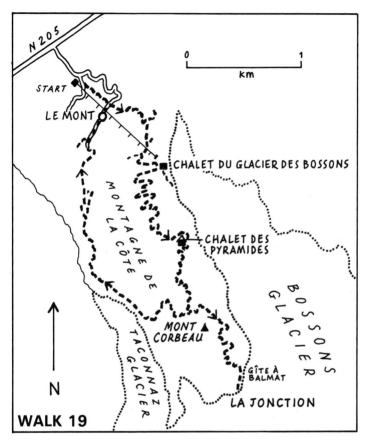

Pyramides – Bec du Corbeau – La Jonction – Taconnaz
moraine – Le Mont

Total ascent: 1433m (4701ft)

Timings: Ascent 4½ hours (deduct ½ hour if using chair-lift); descent
2½ hours.

Meals, snacks and drinks available at Chalet du Glacier des Bossons
and Chalet des Pyamides. Accommodation at Chalet des Pyramides.
*Special note: This route involves a considerable amount of climbing,
so allow plenty of time for breaks. The upper half penetrates a*

*high-mountain environment at the junction of two glaciers, so in addition to normal gear it is advisable to carry spare warm clothing, snow goggles or good sunglasses, suncream and sunhat. Although for most of the way an ice-axe will be superfluous, there are likely to be extensive snowbanks to cross above Mont Corbeau. Obtain a weather forecast before setting out.*

There are few walkers' routes in the Chamonix-Mont-Blanc area more exciting than this one; not just exciting but civilised too, with a couple of refreshment points on the lower stretches! For those eschewing the soft option of a chair-lift ride up the first 400m (1300ft), there is a good deal of leg work to do, but paths, in common with most in the Alps, are superbly graded so that whatever your pace there is never any need to become unduly fatigued.

As the walk unfolds, you will experience a transition from a lush, busy valley to some of the wildest alpine terrain accessible without specialist mountaineering equipment and experience. There are some airy situations but no real difficulties for the competent mountain walker.

In effect, Montagne de la Côte is a finger of land steeply inclined on the flanks of Mont Blanc and whose tip deflects the Bossons and Taconnaz glaciers into their separate downward courses. This same itinerary was used by Jacques Balmat and Dr. Michel Paccard during their successful attempt to be the first to climb Mont Blanc in August 1786. From the route's highest points, the peaks of the Mont Blanc massif take on noticeably different profiles from their remote valley perspectives and to witness at close quarters the great frozen confluence of the Bossons and Taconnaz glaciers is an unforgettable experience.

**Le Mont** is a small settlement south of the busy N506 between Chamonix and Les Houches and stands slightly aloof from the bustle of the valley bottom near the terminal lobe of the Bossons Glacier. If not using the chair-lift which starts below at Grange Neuve near Les Tissières and Les Bossons campsites (car parking, bars etc.), walk up from the bottom station more or less beneath the lift cable (south-east) over rough grassy slopes. Cross the minor access road to Le Mont (more car parking) and continue up, veering left into forest. (There are several paths in the area but keep in the overall direction of the chair-lift.) The path turns right, opens out across grass and finally climbs a stony piste left, to the **Chalet du Glacier des Bossons** (1410m – 4626ft. Meals, snacks and drinks).

*At the Chalet des Pyramides high above the Bossons Glacier*

From the terrace there is a wonderful view down and across the Bossons Glacier and in all probability you will see students from the Glacier School below practising ice-craft on the deeply serrated surface of curving ice ridges. To the right (south-east), a convoluted sea of ice leads the eye right up to the dazzling heights of the Aiguille du Midi and the jagged skyline of the other Chamonix Aiguilles.

The **Bossons Glacier** is noteworthy both for its exceptional steepness (averaging 45 deg.) and consequent rate of flow which is double that of the Mer de Glace; and for the low altitude of its terminal sector, which reaches down through pine forest close to the uppermost buildings in Le Mont. From the Chalet du Glacier, a spur path leads down to an ice-cave carved into the glacier's edge.

To continue the walk, find the path at the back (chair-lift side) of the Chalet, signed 'Chalet des Pyramides and la Jonction'. The ensuing ascent is in the best tradition of alpine paths – easily graded zig-zags in almost constant shade, which can be a blessing if you are going up on a sunny day. Farther up, it curves round the head of a large couloir and these precipitous slopes provide a foretaste of what is to come.

Beyond an astonishingly exposed and solitary tree whose gnarled roots overhang dizzy space, the **Chalet des Pyramides** is reached –

*The Bossons Glacier from dizzy slopes above the Chalet des Pyramides*

(1895m – 6717ft; privately owned; 15 places; guardian during the summer months; reservations contact Mr. Simard, Les Bossons. Meals and drinks are served, though don't expect too much – water is very scarce and the guardian carries food supplies up daily!) There is a viewing point reached by path below the chalet and from anywhere in the vicinity the Bossons Glacier appears more spectacular than ever, contorted by crevasses and ice cliffs.

Perhaps the toughest climbing on the route now follows, first on tight zig-zags up a formidably steep vegetated gully to a narrow ridge, then up rocky slopes, before the gradient eases off and you contour above more beetling drops. For the first time, the **Taconnaz Glacier** is seen clearly as the path diverts to the west flank of **Montagne de la Côte**. From this altitude and position, views are extensive and of unusual verticality.

One disused pylon is passed and a series of zig-zags leads to another one. Just beyond, the original routing (still quoted in some French guidebooks and maps) climbed to the crest of the Bec du Corbeau and proceeded along a short but very exposed rock ridge, before angling down on the Bossons side to a small saddle where the

*Bossons Glacier (left), Mont Blanc du Tacul (top centre) and Mont Maudit (top right) from Montagne de la Côte*

Taconnaz path joined. Serious rockfalls have rendered the ridge highly dangerous and there is a sign to this effect ('Passage Dangereux'). Follow instead the new routing which descends gradually towards the Taconnaz Glacier and meets the Taconnaz path (down which lies our descent) at a signpost. At this junction, turn up left on zig-zags which take you beneath **Mont Corbeau** then over easier angled slopes south-east on a clear path above the Bossons Glacier.

Increasingly snowy (particularly until mid-July) and waymarked occasionally with paint flashes, the route winds up over inclined rocky mountainside in a series of acute twists and turns, to finally arrive at **Gîte à Balmat** (where the famous Jacques Balmat spent much time acquainting himself with the mountain environment and where he and Dr. Michel Paccard camped en route for their historic first ascent of Mont Blanc on August 8th 1786). It is possible to reach **'la Jonction'**, the highest tip of land at 2589m (8494ft), but much depends on conditions and the judgement of individual walkers. In any event, it is inadvisable to stray onto the glacier itself unless you are equipped and have the necessary skills.

Discernible up to the south is the Grands Mulets Refuge (3051m –

10,010ft) on its spine of rock: it is used by present day alpinists on the 'voie normale' up Mont Blanc.

By any yardstick, this is a sensational spot and one to savour. As you gaze out across an ocean of ice, frozen into giant steps and pierced by dark islands of rock ('nunataks'), the Aiguille du Midi rises insistently against the eastern sky, its summit some 1300m (4260ft) higher. To the south-east hangs the blunt, flat-topped snow ridge of Mont Blanc du Tacul and neighbouring Mont Maudit; to the south-west the Dôme and Aiguille de Goûter; and between them, south-south-west from la Jonction, lies Mont Blanc itself.

Descent is by the same route as far as the signpost under Mont Corbeau. Here, either follow the upward path and simply reverse the ascent route, or, for a closer acquaintance with the **Taconnaz Glacier**, turn down left (west). The rugged path loses height in numerous bends to the edge of the moraine which it then follows down, eventually entering patchy forest and crossing the bed of the Corrua torrent. Keep to the central path which soon emerges onto a track and the road end at Le Mont. To reach the start, walk to the chair-lift cable and drop down beneath it over rough grass to the bottom station.

### Walk 20   Lac du Brévent and Aiguillette des Houches

Routing: Le Coupeau – Merlet – Bellachat Refuge – Lac du Brévent
         – Aiguillette des Houches – Chalets de Chailloux – Merlet –
         Le Coupeau

Total ascent: 1135m (3724ft)

Timings: Le Coupeau to Bellachat Refuge – 2¾ hours
         Bellachat Refuge to Lac du Brévent – ½ hour
         Lac du Brévent to Aiguillette des Houches – 1½ hours
         Descent to Le Coupeau – 2¼ hours

Meals, snacks and drinks available at Merlet and the Bellachat Refuge (accom.)

*Special note: The route between the Bellachat Refuge and Lac du Brévent is indistinct and is best not attempted in mist or bad weather by walkers without tried and tested navigational skills: the terrain is rugged, craggy in places and may be partially snow-covered early in the season.*

Though no great linear distance on a map, this walk traverses some of the steepest ground in the Chamonix area and involves a very respectable amount of climbing! The lower sections are in delightful, aromatic pine forest but higher up on this westernmost spur of the

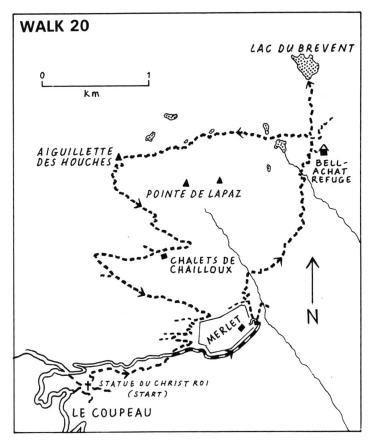

WALK 20

0 [ km ] 1

LAC DU BREVENT

AIGUILLETTE
DES HOUCHES

POINTE DE LAPAZ

BELL-
ACHAT
REFUGE

CHALETS DE
CHAILLOUX

N

MERLET

STATUE DU CHRIST ROI
(START)

LE COUPEAU

Aiguilles Rouges massif, underfoot conditions are as rough as they
come.

Nowhere are there better views of Mont Blanc than on the ascent
beyond Merlet, and this magnificent spectacle is heightened by the
precipitous mountainside to which your path clings, high above the
intervening Arve valley. From Aiguillette des Houches there are
equally fascinating prospects to the north-west, where the great
bastions of cliff fringing the Desert de Platé rise sheer beyond the
Diosaz Gorges.

**Le Chapeau** (1200m – 3937ft), a scattered village, lies approximately 2km north of Les Houches. To the right off the 5th acute hairpin bend in the road can be found limited parking space (an alternative is to park at Merlet Mountain Zoo, where the route can be picked up). A short distance along the track stands the massive, 17m-high statue of **Le Christ Roi**, constructed from reinforced concrete and paid for by donations from locals and tourists in the 1930's.

The ascent to the Bellachat Refuge follows the routing of the Tour du Mont Blanc and the GR5 Traverse of the Alps, so will be clearly waymarked with red and white paint stripes. Climbing from the statue, the trail soon veers right (east) and meanders over avalanche-prone slopes (possible diversions), eventually emerging on the semi-surfaced road leading up to **Merlet Mountain Zoo** (1562m – 5125ft; animals in partial freedom; meals, snacks and drinks; admission charge).

Walk up north off the final access road bend alongside the perimeter fence and keep ahead at a path junction where the fence turns left. Zig-zags follow and climbing begins in earnest! You cross the Lapaz torrent and continue upwards, slanting across vertiginous slopes round little rocky corners, in and out of thin forest. Two sets of tight zig-zags lead up to the Ravin des Vouillourds, a rocky scramble aided with metal rails, whereafter yet more dusty bends take you up to the **Bellachat Refuge** (2151m – 7057ft; privately owned; 30 places; guardian from end-June to end-Sept; reservations tel: (50) 53.43.23; meals, snacks and drinks).

A path leaves north from the refuge up to a signed junction: right goes on to Le Brévent summit, left direct to Aiguillette des Houches. To approach **Lac du Brévent**, however, it is necessary to steer a course virtually due magnetic north, crossing rough mountain terrain of grass, stones and rock (and possible snow patches). In some 500m the lake is reached, its setting both wild and stunningly beautiful, cradled in a hollow beneath the tortuous rock mass of Le Brévent.

Retrace steps to the path junction above Bellachat Refuge and turn right (west) over undulating ground, past several little streams and marshy ponds behind the Aiguillette du Brévent and Pointe de Lapaz which temporarily conceal Mont Blanc. The way climbs more determinedly half-way along and rises over possible snow to the **Aiguillette des Houches** (2285m – 7497ft). Although a fine ridge falls away to the west, this top is the last significant feature of the Aiguilles Rouges massif before it is cleft by the Diosaz Gorges near Servoz. From the small col, very steep zig-zags requiring care descend to

*Lac du Brévent (right) and Aiguillette des Houches (top right)*

the south then south-west, after which gentler gradients lead over pleasant high pasture to a sharp turn right (west) and the **Chalets de Chaillouz**. Continue on the gradually descending path which enters pine forest and veers back south-east. Ignoring a turn off right (west), you drop through more forest to reach the perimeter fence of Merlet Mountain Zoo. Here turn right and keep on down left past several junctions in zig-zags, finally reaching the zoo's access road. By reversing the initial leg of this itinerary, the starting point near Le Christ Roi statue is soon attained.

## Walk 21   Col de Voza, Mont-Lachat and Le Nid d'Aigle

Routing: Les Houches – Col de Voza – Bellevue – Mont-Lachat – Le
Nid d'Aigle – Chalet de l'Are – Bellevue – Les Houches
Total ascent: 1364m (4475ft)
Timings: Les Houches to Col de Voza – 2 hours
Col de Voza to Le Nid d'Aigle – 2 hours
Descent to Bellevue – 1½ hours
Bellevue to Les Houches via Col de Voza – 1½ hours
Meals, snacks, drinks and accommodation available at Col de Voza,
Bellevue and Le Nid d'Aigle (no accom.)
*Special note: Although much of the walk is over easy terrain, the
ascent of Mont-Lachat is by a very steep path. The section from Le Nid
d'Aigle to the Bionnassay Glacier moraine is rugged and likely to be
snow-covered in places early in the summer. Both potential
difficulties, however, are readily avoided if needs be by amending the
itinerary – suggestions in the text.*

A climb of over 1300m and subsequent descent makes for a fairly
strenuous day out, but it is always satisfying to reach a respectable
altitude under your own steam right from the valley floor. However,
perhaps more than on any other walk in this region, mechanical
transport is always relatively close at hand, so that should time,
weather or other circumstance suggest taking a ride either on the
ascent or descent, your route can be varied accordingly. Indeed,
there are enough possible permutations of walking and riding to
satisfy most eventualities.

Forestry activity seems more evident on the hillsides south of Les
Houches than elsewhere in the Chamonix valley, and even well
established walking trails are not immune to the ravages of
bulldozers and felling operations. (The author can vouch for this
personally, having spent a frustrating and ultimately fruitless day
prospecting a route up to Col du Mont Lachat via the Dangereux
chalets. Steep mud banks and broken trees had replaced map paths
and the only way remaining through impenetrable undergrowth lay
up a crudely bulldozed track to Col de Voza! It is hoped that readers
will be spared such experiences, though in truth the routing
described below to Col de Voza should be intact as it is on several
important long-distance trails.)

This walk offers a gradual transition from valley floor through
meadows and forest to Col de Voza, then on up increasingly open
and rugged mountainside to a vantage point overlooking the
Bionassay Glacier and its encircling peaks. It is possible to shorten

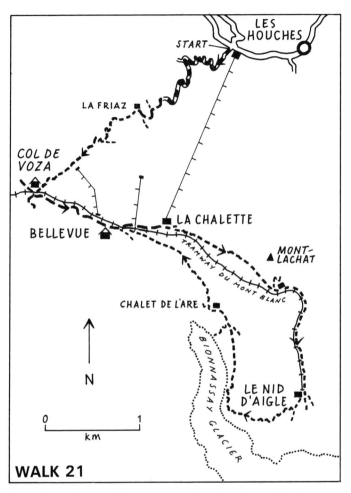

**WALK 21**

the day by taking a cable-car between Les Houches and Bellevue, or by catching the rack-and-pinion Tramway du Mont Blanc (TMB) between Col de Voza and Le Nid d'Aigle (Eagle's Nest). Last cable-car 5.30pm. Last tram down 5.30pm (1st July to 7th Sept.)

Running up from Le Fayet and St. Gervais-les-Bains to the north-west, the TMB was originally intended to reach the summit of

Mont Blanc – naïvely perhaps, considering the hostile and exposed high-mountain terrain, yet typical of the audacity shown by engineers earlier this century. Its development coincided with the establishment of two observatories on Mont Blanc around 1900.

A footpath accompanies the tramway from Col de Voza up to the top station at Le Nid d'Aigle, so navigation on this stretch presents no problem, however bad the visibility! As you gain altitude, extensive views open up down towards Val Montjoie and across to the Bionnassay Glacier, bounded to the south by the Aiguilles de Bionassay and Tricot. From the walk's highest point, a descent leads towards the glacier's lateral moraine and thence along steep, vegetated slopes above Bionnassay village to Bellevue. It is sobering to remember July 1892 when a huge mudslide swept down from the glacier's snout, scouring the steep little valley of the Bionnassay torrent and completely obliterating Bionnay village. Over 200 lives were lost.

**Les Houches** is one of the area's most attractive towns, set back above the busy road and railway and altogether less frenetic a place than Chamonix in high season. There are all shops, services and types of accommodation to be found here and the walk begins from the Bellevue cable-car station car park.

Walk about 100m west along the road and turn left up a track. Waymarking to Col de Voza also includes the long-distance GR5 and Tour du Mont Blanc trails – red and white – but is not always in evidence when you need it! The track climbs through woods, past chalets and up to a metalled lane at a hotel/restaurant. Turn left and keep ahead at some chalets when the lane becomes a track between railings. There are magnificent views back along the Chamonix valley and the great wall of peaks and glaciers on its right.

Keep right at a fork, pass La Friaz hut, and just before a bulldozed area ahead, turn left into forest and follow the steadily rising path to meadows and the **Col de Voza** (1653m – 5423ft). There is a welcome bar/hotel (accommodation) and a halt for the TMB (tramway). Cross the line and follow the track up left to **Bellevue** (1794m – 5886ft. TMB halt). The privately owned hotel serves meals, snacks and drinks, has 30 beds and is open all year round – this is also popular winter skiing country. Ahead and dazzlingly high rises the snowy Aiguille de Bionnassay.

Continue along the easy path, crossing to the left of the tramway to reach the hotel/café at **La Chalette** (Snacks, drinks, top station of cable-car from Les Houches, TMB halt). If you're feeling less than

*Walkers near Bellevue. Bionnassay Glacier and Aiguille above right*

energetic, the tramway can simply be followed up to Col du Mont Lachat and Le Nid d'Aigle on a good flanking path.

The forward route for this walk (not recommended in wet conditions) now takes the path through bushes just to the right of La Chalette café terrace. It climbs determinedly through alder trees and is provided with a metal cable to haul on where necessary, before emerging onto open grassy slopes where, if anything, the gradient increases! After a false top, a short extra pull up brings you to the gentle grassy eastern flank of **Mont-Lachat**, whose actual summit (2115m – 6939ft) lies a little way off to the left. Views north-east down over the Chamonix valley are surprisingly airy.

By following the path onwards, **Col du Mont Lachat** (TMB tram halt) is attained, its private cable-car top station buildings untidily derelict – an odd sight in this area of thriving tourism. The tramway track is now closely shadowed as it slants up for over a kilometre, past two short tunnels, to **Le Nid d'Aigle** (2372m – 7782ft), terminus of the tramway (meals, snacks, drinks). Aiguille de Bionnassay still dominates, below it the chaotic surface of the Bionnassay Glacier. This high spot of the walk is used as a point of departure for ascents in the area and to reach the Tête Rousse Refuge up to the east.

Take a path off right (south-west then generally west) from the TMB station. There may well be snowbanks to cross, and on some steeper, rougher sections the path has been improved, though it is still a rugged one. Eventually it swings north and drops in zig-zags to a broad grassy valley. Just before **Chalet de l'Are**, you join the Tour du Mont Blanc variant. Ignore a path down left and thereafter stay around the same height along vegetated but precipitous hillside, whose slope eases back on entering woods and shortly after leads out to Bellevue.

Much will depend on the time of day, weather and your inclination as to which mode of descent is chosen. Purists will reverse the upward walk by returning to Les Houches on foot via Col de Voza; for others, the cable-car from La Chalette may prove too tempting to resist!

## Walk 22   Le Prarion from Les Houches

Routing: Les Houches – Col de Voza – Le Prarion – Col de la Forclaz
       – Granges des Chavants – Les Houches
Total ascent: 976m (3202ft)
Timings: Les Houches to Col de Voza – 2 hours
        Col de Voza to Le Prarion – 40 min.
        Le Prarion to Les Houches via Col de la Forclaz – 2 hours
Meals, snacks, drinks and accommodation available at Col de Voza and Hôtel du Prarion.

This itinerary is twinned with Walk 25, and ascends Le Prarion from its other, eastern, side. Walkers based in the Chamonix valley may choose this ascent, since the detour round to Val Montjoie is a lengthy one and unless further walks in that area are contemplated

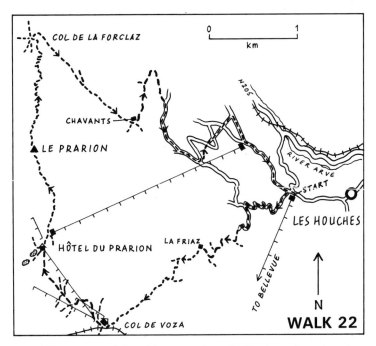

Map labels: COL DE LA FORCLAZ, CHAVANTS, LE PRARION, HÔTEL DU PRARION, LA FRIAZ, COL DE VOZA, SOUZN, RIVER ARVE, START, LES HOUCHES, TO BELLEVUE, N, **WALK 22**, 0 1 km

would be a waste of time. For notes about Le Prarion, please turn to Walk 25.

Forestry management on the hillsides above Les Houches seems to result in more disruption to walking trails than elsewhere in the Chamonix valley, so even important map-marked paths are subject to change from time to time. However, it is hoped that the main walking route from Les Houches to Col de Voza (part of the TMB and GR5 long-distance treks) will correspond with the direction given below.

**Les Houches** manages to stand somewhat aloof from the bustle of the Chamonix valley, though it contains all shops, services and types of accommodation. The walk starts at the Bellevue cable-car station car park, 750m west of the town centre.

100m farther west along the road, turn left up a track. Waymarking to Col de Voza – red and white – is not always there when needed! The track climbs through woods, past chalets and up to a metalled

*The Desert de Platé viewed from Le Prarion*

lane at a hotel/restaurant. Turn left and keep ahead at some chalets when the lane becomes a track between railings. There are magnificent views back along the Chamonix valley and the great wall of peaks and glaciers on its right.

Keep right at a fork, pass La Friaz hut, and just before a cleared area ahead, turn left into forest and follow the steadily rising path to meadows and the **Col de Voza** (1653m – 5423ft; bar/hotel offering meals, snacks, drinks and accommodation; Tramway du Mont Blanc halt.) Emerging from forest to confront an uninterrupted vista of snowy summits and glaciers to the south and east is one of walk's most exciting moments.

Without crossing the tramway, turn half-right (north-west), away from the large hotel/bar and up a good track beneath ski-lifts, waymarked blue/yellow. (Ignore the track off right, which rises before descending to the valley). The broad track winds up over grassy slopes popular with winter skiers, past turnings off left and right, and reaches the **Hôtel du Prarion** (1853m – 6079ft; privately owned; 30 places; permanently open; meals, snacks and drinks; nearby viewing table).

Continue ahead to the cabin-lift top station, walk alongside the building, then strike off left (north), whereafter the way is indicated with red paint flashes. Climbing pleasantly past alpenrose and dwarf conifers, the path mounts a rocky step at a small col and follows the ridge to its summit – **Le Prarion** (1969m – 6460ft). Throughout this easy ascent, views are excellent, culminating in a 360deg. panorama from the little trig. point.

This is indeed a vantage point of great quality and well worth the effort to reach it. Many well known features will be seen from a different angle, while the overall sense of elevation is considerably greater than one would expect from a modest summit. Scanning west from Mont Blanc itself lie the Bionnassay Glacier and surrounding peaks, farther west Col du Bonhomme and Mont Joly, round to Sallanches and the Autoroute Blanche in a much broader valley than Chamonix's, unconfined by high mountain walls. To the north and north-east are the Desert de Platé, Rochers des Fiz and Col d'Anterne, and an end-on profile of the Aiguilles Rouges.

The onward route proceeds north but now twists and zig-zags down the precipitous, vegetated end of the Prarion ridge towards the symmetrical, wooded cone of Tête Noire. A metal cable adds security past a few particularly exposed metres, but then it is downhill with a vengeance, over the occasional scrambly rock step, the apparently impassable steepnesses negotiated easily by the path's devious progress. Woodland grows ever more luxuriant as height is lost and soon a forestry track is reached, leading on to a wide, rather muddy clearing in pine forest – **Col de la Forclaz** (1532m – 5026ft). (Forestry work in this area might affect future routing in the immediate vicinity of the col).

Turn right (east), rather ambiguously waymarked white to 'Les Houches par les terrains' and 'Charrouse'. (Don't take the left fork which goes down to Vaudagne).

The bulldozed forestry track, quite steep, makes a bee-line for Les Houches but after a while bends away sharp left. Here you take the more overgrown track ahead at the corner, go past a pumping station and through woods, over small streams, past an electricity pylon, to rise slightly and reach barns at **Granges des Chavants**.

Follow the track on downhill, keeping right at a junction near chalets, and at the road at La Côte turn right, along past various buildings until you come to a road intersection beneath the Prarion cabin-lift. Here turn left then immediately right down a path signed 'Les Houches' past chalets to a road. Cross over and continue down, crossing the next road too and walking past farm buildings and a drinking water pipe. At the next road, turn right, pass the Prarion cabin-lift station and continue forward through Le Fouillis to the Bellevue cable-car car park where the walk began.

**Suggested shorter walks in the Chamonix area**

## LE CHAPEAU AND MER DE GLACE VIEWPOINT
Total ascent: 359m (1178ft) – 2¼ hours' walking

Le Lavancher is a charming old village set above the busy valley between Chamonix and Argentière and reached on a by-road just north of Les Tines. The road gives way to a twisting track (car parking) which can be short-cut to the right. At the top, the walk turns right off the Chemin du Mauvais Pas towards Le Chapeau. Ignore paths off right to the Arveyron Gorge and left to Croix de Lognan, continuing upwards (south-east) on steep slopes and out of forest. There is a small waterfall in the Chapeau torrent, after which the way climbs zig-zags over moraine topped with larch trees to Le Chapeau chalet (1576m – 5171ft; refreshments).

15mins farther on at the moraine edge under the old Mauvais Pas track is the abandoned 'Pointe de Vue de la Mer de Glace', rendered obsolete by the significant retreat of the Mer de Glace in recent years. There is still much fine alpine scenery in all directions, however, which takes in the Arveyron Gorge, the Chamonix Aiguilles and the Arve valley. Descent is by the same route.

## THE ROCHERS DES MOTTETS VIEWPOINT
Total ascent: 558m (1831ft) – 3 hours' walking

Level ground between the Arveyron torrent and the River Arve to the north of Chamonix is occupied by Les Praz de Chamonix and a number of campsites. The village of Les Bois lies to the east of this area.

The walk begins from the east of the village, enters forest and crosses the Arveyron on the 'Pont-himalayen'. Veer right (south-west) over a track and onto Chemin de la Filia which climbs through forest and after two acute bends joins a good level track (from Chamonix). Turn left (east) and continue along out of forest, past a path right to Montenvers, and up over rocky slopes to the Rochers des Mottets viewpoint (1638m – 5374ft).

This magnificent spot overlooks not only the Mer de Glace (see Walk 15), but also the Aiguilles des Drus, a dramatic spur falling from Aiguille Verte. Whilst it is possible to proceed further (south-east) down to the glacier edge, care is needed as there is some danger from rock and ice fall. Return to Les Bois is by the same route.

## CASCADE DU DARD

Total ascent: 200m (656ft) – 2½ hours' walking

A stony track connects the large Aiguille du Midi cable-car car park, south of the Chamonix by-pass, with Les Molliasses campsite. Follow the track up left (south) to the 'Maison Forestière', just beyond which will be found the Plan de l'Aiguille path. Take this path but in the opposite direction (south-west) to a hairpin bend in the Mont Blanc Tunnel access road. Walk up the road for about 50m and turn off left, climbing more steeply at first in forest. You are joined near the next road hairpin (now separated by the Favrands torrent) by the path from Les Pélerins and in a short distance come to a footbridge down to the right over the Dard torrent. Nearby is a buvette (1233m – 4045ft) and a beautiful viewpoint of the Dard waterfall above. (NOTE: The chalet building is susceptible to avalanche damage: an enquiry at Chamonix's Tourist Office will confirm whether refreshments are available at the time of your visit.)

To vary the return if desired, cross the footbridge and turn right (south-east) on a fairly steep but well graded path zig-zagging up through forest. At the first path junction, turn down left. The easy descent (keep straight on at an intersection) grows steeper towards the valley, but eventually emerges at the eastern end of the Aiguille du Midi car park.

## CHALET DE CERRO AND THE PLATEAU DES PYRA-MIDES

Total ascent: 526m (1726ft) – 3 hours' walking

Leave from the car park on the right and before the Mont Blanc Tunnel portal. The path to Chalet de Cerro climbs an embankment and enters forest on easy gradients to the Crosette torrent which is crossed on a footbridge. Joined soon by a path up from Les Bossons, you climb zig-zags and arrive at the Chalet de Cerro (1358m – 4455ft). Despite the chalet's ease of access and modest elevation, there are truly magnificent views over the Bossons Glacier from this moraine, including the steep mountainsides opposite (see Walk 19). A 'crèmerie' provides refreshments.

Immediately above the chalet building, take the shady path which crosses the Crosette torrent and winds up through delightful forest to the upper limit of trees. The final 200m or so of this route are over glacial moraine and the path is consequently much rougher. However, here at the top of the 'Plateau des Pyramides' (1800m – 5905ft) are sensational seracs and ice cliffs seen at close quarters. Descent is by the same route.

# 4:
# Servoz and
# Plateau d'Assy

*Col d'Anterne (top right) and the Lower Arve Valley
from Le Prarion*

**Walk 23   Col d'Anterne**

Routing: Plaine Joux – Chalet-Refuge de Barmus – Chalets d'Ayères – Col d'Anterne – Chalet-hôtel Moëde-Anterne – Chalets du Souay (variant via Lac de Pormenaz) – Lac Vert – Plaine Joux

Total ascent: 947m (3107ft)

Timings: Plaine Joux to Col d'Anterne – 3½ hours

Col d'Anterne to Chalets du Souay via Chalet-hôtel Moëde-Anterne – 2 hours (2½ hours via Lac de Pormenaz)

Chalets du Souay to Plaine Joux – 1½ hours

Meals, snack, drinks and accommodation available at Plaine Joux, Chalet-Refuge de Barmus (accom. only), Chalet-hôtel Moëde-Anterne, Le Chatelet (no accom.) and Lac Vert (no accom.)

*Special note: The variant from Chalet-hôtel Moëde Anterne to Chalets du Souay via Lac de Pormenaz presents more in the way of problems for walkers than the main routing, but is more varied. First, the path to Lac de Pormenaz is boggy in places and not always clear (especially early in the season in melting snow); second, the descent from the lake is by way of a very steep path with rock steps and is not recommended in wet conditions.*

The walk's principal destination is Col d'Anterne, one of the premier viewpoints over the Mont Blanc range, from Aiguille du Midi in the east to Aiguille de Goûter in the west. In fact, the massif is several linear kilometres away, with Le Brévent interposed in the middle distance, yet the sight of that snowy dome of peaks culminating in Europe's highest summit is in no way diminished. For those fortunate enough to have clear visibility, it is a thrilling and unforgettable panorama.

The outward leg follows the base of a great bastion of cliffs and steep scree slopes which run east from Pointe de Platé (2554m – 8379ft) to Pointe d'Anterne (2733m – 8966ft). Only in one place – Passage de Derechoir – is this formidable barrier penetrated by a walking route, an arduous one threatened by rock-fall. However, despite its proximity to such a grandiose natural feature, this itinerary stays on good paths and tracks throughout, largely in the Passy Nature Reserve.

The Chalet-hôtel Moëde-Anterne stands below Col d'Anterne near the source of the Souay torrent and is justifiably popular. For the first part of the return leg, there is a choice between two alternatives, the one via Lac de Pormenaz over more difficult terrain at times. Lac Vert, a beauty spot accessible by road and not far from

147

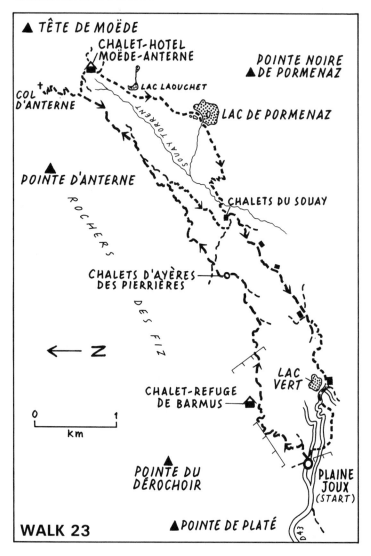

▲ TÊTE DE MOËDE

CHALET-HOTEL
MOËDE-ANTERNE

POINTE NOIRE
▲ DE PORMENAZ

COL
D'ANTERNE

LAC LAOUCHET

LAC DE PORMENAZ

SOUAY TORRENT

▲ POINTE D'ANTERNE

CHALETS DU SOUAY

ROCHERS

CHALETS D'AYÈRES
DES PIERRIÈRES

DES FIZ

← N

LAC
VERT

0        1
km

CHALET-REFUGE
DE BARMUS

POINTE DU
DÉROCHOIR

PLAINE
JOUX
(START)

WALK 23

▲ POINTE DE PLATÉ

D43

the finish, provides an interesting conclusion. The walk is a long one, but refreshment points are conveniently spaced and much of the going is easy.

Plaine Joux, a developing winter skiing resort, is approximately 5km by the D43 road north-east of Plateau-d'Assy. In effect, it stands high on a broad natural shelf between the moderately industrial Arve valley and a long line of cliffs to the north, above which and unseen from below lies a vast limestone upland – the Desert de Platé (see Walk 24).

**Plaine Joux**, at 1360m (4462ft) altitude, contains a few bars, restaurants and hotels and an Information Centre for the Passy Nature Reserve. There is limited-facility camping on open ground (apply at 'Le Ranch' snack bar) and oodles of parking space. Being somewhat off the beaten track, this corner of the Chamonix area is much quieter, though the nearest shops and services are at Plateau-d'Assy.

To the right of 'Le Ranch' snack bar terrace will be found a cluster of walkers' signs (rather misleadingly aligned!). Walk up to the right of a corrugated-iron roofed chalet on a stony track and keep up right to a sign for 'Ecole d'escalade' (Climbing School) at a bend. Red and yellow waymarks cropping up often on this route are for the Tour du Pays du Mont-Blanc. Keep round left and soon the beetling grey precipices leading up to Pointe de Platé impose their presence ahead, a presence maintained for much of the walk.

At a clearing and track intersection, take a left turn to a boulder inscribed 'Moutons – chiens en laisse obligatoire', and swing right to another similarly painted rock imploring owners to keep Rover on a lead! You now veer back left uphill. (At the time of writing, road building is in progress hereabouts which could change path routings). Continue up beneath a ski-lift and almost immediately turn right, back under it as the gradient eases.

A drinking water stand pipe is passed and shortly after you reach the **Chalet-Refuge de Barmus** (1610m – 5282ft; privately owned, 20 places; guardian during the summer period. Reservations tel. M. Bernard Gruz – (50) 78.25.35 or (50) 78.30.72.) Above the attractive buildings soar the jutting, prow-like buttresses of the Rochers des Fiz. Just to the right are a waymarking post and picnic table above a magnificent view down past Lac Vert to the Sallanches plain 1000m (3300ft) below, and beyond to a wide horizon of mountains.

The track now levels off, allowing contemplation in more detail of the towers, buttresses and striated cliffs up to the left. Beyond a

149

*Chalet-refuge de Barmus and the Rochers des Fiz*

ski-lift and a chaos of rocky outcrops and boulders, the way continues
in similar vein, past a path right to Le Chatelet and Lac Vert (a
short-cut back to the start). You soon arrive at **Chalets d'Ayères des
Pierrières** (1630m – 5348ft), a small chalet development amongst the
boulders and served by jeep tracks.

There appears to be a steady growth in the colonisation of

mountain land, both by the winter skiing industry and to satisfy an apparent urge in those who can afford it to own holiday homes wherever 4-wheel-drive access can be bulldozed through. The effect is a spreading blight of unsightly tracks and construction activity, noticed most of all by the summer walker who encounters it devoid of a disguising snow cover.

Ahead are various waymark signs, including the 'Chalet-hôtel au Col d'Anterne'. A notice also permits 4-wheel-drive vehicles to reach this hut on the rough track and asks drivers to give consideration to walkers. In fact, vehicular use is minimal in the author's experience. The only path to attack the cliff barrier slants back left (north-west) up to the Passage de Derechoir, scene of a catastrophic rock-fall in 1751. Similar rock-falls have occurred as recently as 1976 on the Rochers des Fiz. The track down right (south-east) provides a short-cut to Chalets du Souay.

From now on, paths short-cut the jeep track's dog-leg bends and are marked here and there with yellow paint spots. As you cross torrent beds at the head of the Ravin des Monthieux, the intimidating steepnesses of the Rochers des Fiz loom closer overhead, culminating in the now discernible Pointe d'Anterne.

Out on grassy slopes littered with boulders and rock-falls, the track continues past a little cabin under a boulder (NOTE: unless the variant via Lac de Pormenaz is taken, the return leg of this walk comes back to this point before diverging down right, so it is useful to

*Mont Blanc and Le Brévent (lower left) from Col d'Anterne*

make a mental note of this location). The track undulates along rugged mountainside, crossing numerous torrent beds and gaining height gradually. Where it drops towards the Chalet-hôtel, keep up left. About 300m (1000ft) of fairly stiff ascent, mostly on zig-zags. leads up to **Col d'Anterne** (2257 – 7405ft).

This wide saddle with its crucifix between Pointe d'Anterne and Tête de Moëde not only overlooks Mont Blanc in all its shining splendour, but also affords interesting views north towards the limestone pre-alps of the Chablais and the continuation of the Fiz cliffs up to Tête à l'Âne. For walkers on the long-distance GR5 Traverse of the Alps, this col represents a transition into the high granite mountains around Mont Blanc; their approach from the north will probably have been over quite extensive snowfields.

Descending from the col, follow waymarks down to the popular **Chalet-hôtel Moëde-Anterne**, which advertises itself locally as offering peaceful stays 'away from it all'. At 2002m (6568ft), it is privately owned, with resident guardian through the summer, and provides meals, snacks and drinks as well as accommodation (tel: 93.60.43). Once a more traditional refuge, jeep track access and new management have extended its hospitality to non-walkers too.

(*Variant to Chalets du Souay*: This rather more testing alternative is not recommended in mist or wet weather. Leave south-west from the Chalet-hôtel, at first on the well-walked GR5 path, and after about 200m fork off right to the diminutive Laouchet lake. Proceed ahead in a generally south-south-west direction on a sometimes poorly defined path over marshy, undulating terrain to reach the north shore of **Lac de Pormenaz** beneath two smaller lakes and a knoll. Rearing 400m (1300ft) above is Pointe Noire de Pormenaz.

Walk along the lake's west shore, over its outlet stream, and follow a thin path down south-west into the deepening cleft of **Le Chordre**. The subsequent descent is very steep in places and rocky steps need care as the path loses altitude rapidly over vegetated slopes to the Souay torrent emerging from a gorge. Cross on a footbridge and head up through drifts of wild flowers to the chalet buildings and jeep track at **Le Souay**.)

The **main route** from the Chalet-hôtel Moëde-Anterne follows the outward track back to the boulder cabin. Just below will be found a rock waymarked 'Souay' with an arrow pointing downhill. This unpromising start (not shown on maps) soon becomes a well-made path zig-zagging steeply down to rough pasture. It crosses a torrent near a waterfall and descends, muddily in places, to the jeep track some way below the Chalets d'Ayères des Pierrières which will be recognised from the outward walk.

Go down the track, veering right (south-west) at **Chalets du Souay** and continue via Chalets d'Ayères en Bas to **Le Guet**. Farther on, there are refreshments at **Le Chatelet** and 30m beyond, we turn down left on a path waymarked yellow and Lac Vert. Passing through mixed woodland, height is lost quickly down shaley ground. Keep left at a shaley landslip and in 100m keep straight on, eventually coming down to **Lac Vert** (car parking, bar/restaurant, crêperie, ice-creams and pizzas!) Lac Vert itself is a delectable circle of dark green water surrounded by picturesque rocks and, it should be said, the adjacent tourist development is generally in good taste!

To end this lengthy outing, walk west up the motor road but before the first bend turn off left onto a good track, which takes you through delightful open pine forest and emerges at ski-lifts and the road. Plaine Joux is along to the left.

## Walk 24   Desert de Platé and the Platé Refuge

Routing: Praz-Coutant – Ugine torrent – Refuge de Platé – optional
          extension to Col du Colonney – return by same route.

Total ascent: 812m (2664ft); or 1101m (3612ft) to Col du Colonney.

Timings: Ascent – 2 to 2½ hours
            Descent – 1½ hours
            (Allow an extra 1¾ hours for the Col du Colonney
            extension).

Meals, snacks, drinks and accommodation available at the Platé Refuge.

*Special note: Although the path is airy and steep in places and its course rather intimidating from below, it can be safely negotiated by experienced walkers with a normal degree of care. It is advisable to obtain a weather forecast before setting out, as mist and/or rain will add to the hazards of the route and considerably reduce its attractiveness.*

An ascent to the Platé Refuge is as thrilling a route as any contained in this guidebook. As the River Arve drops west out of the Chamonix valley towards Sallanches, it is bounded to the north by grey, precipitous rock walls 10km in length and up to 700m (2300ft) high. To the mountain walker, this barrier appears utterly impregnable, yet in one or two places a path exploits a line of weakness and permits access to the extraordinary Desert de Platé.

This limestone upland, fissured and eroded by the elements, is devoid of any vegetation save grass and flowers. In some places it so

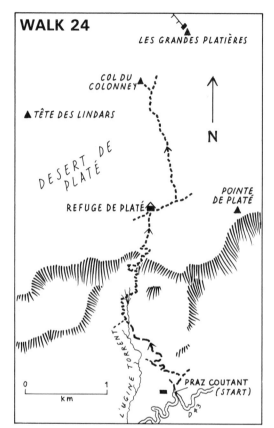

**WALK 24**

LES GRANDES PLATIÈRES

COL DU COLONNEY

▲ TÊTE DES LINDARS

DÉSERT DE PLATÉ

REFUGE DE PLATÉ

POINTE DE PLATÉ

N

L'UGINE TORRENT

0       1
    km

PRAZ COUTANT
(START)

D43

resembles the Yorkshire Dales that you can feel momentarily disorientated, as if a corner of Britain had somehow been grafted onto an alpine landscape; in others, the scale of its limestone peaks and ridges leaves you in no doubt as to your true whereabouts.

Even the reassurances of the printed page may leave some walkers sceptical as to the feasibility of a walkers' route through such forbidding cliffs when viewed from below. There is no denying the way is relentlessly steep and increasingly airy, yet somehow the path manages to surmount each succeeding impasse with cunning zig-zags until you are drawn up against the highest walls, into a cleft, round a

*The Mont Blanc range from the Desert de Platé*

shoulder and suddenly deposited into a horizontal – even pastoral – world, where sheep may be grazing before a dazzling panorama of the Mont Blanc massif. And should the weather be smiling, there will be time to explore further and make an ascent of Col du Colonney.

**Plateau d'Assy** is a small town on the well settled slopes rising from the Arve valley towards the Desert de Platé. Its amenities include all shops, Post Office, hotels, Information Centre and an interesting church. Camping can be found at Passy, Chedde and up at Plaine Joux (see Walk 23).

This walk begins at **Praz-Coutant**, 4km north-east on the D43. It is principally a sanatorium, one of several in this area which seems to be noted for its curative air, though a mere 3km as the crow flies down to the south-east stands a factory belching forth unspeakable pollution! There is some road and track-side parking near the start.

The start itself can be identified easily from the road hairpin bend by spotting a crucifix and signs for Refuge de Platé. Go along this track, following bends right then left and passing a memorial to the victims of an accident on Roc des Fiz (cliffs to the east) in 1970. Take the path along the top of a grassy avalanche protection bank, short-cutting the track. Platé is clearly signed. The track now twists up very pleasantly through woodland, passes a ruin and reaches the **Ugine torrent** (drinkable!) which is crossed on a plank bridge.

Almost straight away you fork right on a path waymarked

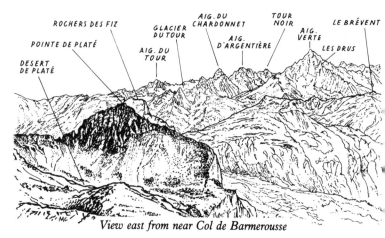

ROCHERS DES FIZ

AIG.DU
CHARDONNET

GLACIER
DU TOUR

TOUR
NOIR

LE BRÉVENT

POINTE DE PLATÉ

AIG.DU
TOUR

AIG.
D'ARGENTIÈRE

AIG.
VERTE

DESERT
DE PLATÉ

LES DRUS

*View east from near Col de Barmerousse*

'Colonney, Desert de Platé' and settle down to a steady rhythm zig-zagging up vegetated, stony mountainside beneath the rock walls which now totally dominate the visible horizon, from Aiguille de Varan left, to Pointe de Platé right. On this lower section of the climb, the path crosses 3 bouldery torrent beds (dry except during late spring thaws or heavy storms), re-crossing one higher up.

Approaching the first cliffs, the way grows more rugged and broken but remains well graded. You come into close proximity with strange friable, horizontal striations, and there is a naturally eroded rock arch to the right at one point. Never was there a more incongruous sign than one which is passed hereabouts – 'Flocks of sheep, keep dogs on lead'. However, the creatures do, in fact, use this path during the annual *transhumance* to higher pastures.

A dauntingly impressive vertical gully up to the right forms the unlikely key to the ascent route as you mount ever-steeper slopes in tight zig-zags over dark, shaley ground right into the dark and dripping recesses of the cleft. High above, the sky shines through a thin slit between rock walls. The path soon veers left above an unguessably airy drop, rounds a buttress, crosses a short artificial ledge constructed to bridge a landslipped impasse and reaches the plateau by turning right over easy slopes.

The transition from sweeping verticality to an almost intimate limestone landscape could hardly be drawn more sharply: it is quite another world! Pale grey, fluted rock alternates with springy turf, the basin ahead rising on both flanks to its enclosing ridges, while to the

156

south there is a sensational view beyond the plateau lip to the Mont Blanc massif. 5 mins away stand the buildings of the **Platé Refuge** (2032m – 6667ft. Club Alpin Français; 40 places; guardian during the summer months, 10 places in winter. Meals, snacks and drinks. Reservations tel. 47.20.08).

Renovated in 1972 and kept supplied by helicopter and cable-lift, the refuge is a small, homely place set in a natural hollow between Pointe de Platé and the Aiguilles de Véran and run by the friendliest people. Acidity in the rain and snow falling on the surrounding Desert de Platé has dissolved the limestone into typical 'clints' and 'grikes' (levels and clefts), and has formed some larger, gorge-like features in a few locations, notably to the north-west; underground watercourses emerge from the plateau edge.

Although not recommended in mist, an extension up to Col du Colonney can be made if weather and time permit by following blue and white waymarks from behind the refuge, first east-north-east then branching off left (north). This is also a variant of the GR96 long-distance trail, waymarked red and white. For most of the hour-long ascent, you are on grassy terrain and waymarks are scarce. Higher up, about 200m beyond a marshy depression, keep left (just north of west) up to **Col du Colonney** (2321m – 7615ft).

There can be little doubt as to what lies beyond to the north – prime winter skiing country. Numerous ski-lifts rise across the denuded rock of summer from the direction of Flaine, a popular resort. It is connected by cable-car to Les Grandes Platières, a top 1km north-east from the col.

Back at the Platé Refuge, make sure to return to the correct point of departure for the descent off the plateau (left of the cable-lift pylon), especially in mist or rain, either of which also makes for very slippery going over limestone. The ascent route is now simply reversed down to Praz-Coutant.

**Suggested shorter walks in the Servoz area**
THE DIOSAZ GORGE
Total ascent: 306m (1004ft) – 1¼ hours' walking

This dramatic natural feature is of great interest and lies just to the east of Servoz. Cross the bridge over the Diosaz and walk left (north) to the entrance, information display and buvette. A fee is payable but seems fully justifiable since each year the footbridges which allow walkers access to the gorge, and the footpath itself, are prone to serious damage from ice, snow and rockfall, necessitating hazardous repair work.

The way is clear throughout the 1½km of its length, insinuating itself between sheer rock walls in the narrow defile. Detailed information is available at the entrance, but amongst the sights are 7 waterfalls and a natural bridge formed by a massive rock which fell during the 16th century and remains lodged 47m (154ft) above the Diosaz torrent.

## CAMP DU CHATELARD
Total ascent: 126m (413ft) – 1½ hours' walking
Vieux-Servoz is the starting point for this walk, which proceeds south-west on a minor road, crossing the River Arve just above a small dam. A path turns off right (west) here, climbing across the wooded flanks of Les Gures to a viewing point at 940m (3084ft). On this plateau are signs of an ancient Celtic settlement and by walking around the site it is possible to see the remains of hut foundations and standing stones – the so-called Pierre du Sacrifice, Dolmen du Laby and La Table. Return by the same route.

## CHÂTEAU SAINT-MICHEL AND LA TRAPPE
Total ascent: 286m (938ft) – 3 hours' walking
South of Servoz, the Pont de l'Avenue leads across the River Arve to Le Lac village. Walk south past the Chapel St. Jean (near the river) and in 250m turn left at the road bend to climb the rocky, wooded hill ahead. At its summit stand the ruins of Château Saint-Michel, dating from around 1300, though the tower and one wall are all that remain.

The onward path descends to a much more recent ruin – that of a disused electricity generating station! Cross the River Arve on the Pont Pélissier to the left and almost immediately turn right (south) where a track leads to a path rising left (south-east) between landslip debris and forest. Zig-zags follow and you veer left (north) past stony slopes and a rocky passage to a mid-height plateau. More bends lead up to La Trappe (1020m – 3346ft), after which the path begins to descend.

Keep right at a path junction, climbing again gradually to cross the Ruisseau des Trois by a small waterfall and reach the road-end at Montvauthier. Follow it down, but short-cut all its long dog-leg bends on a clear path dropping directly to a riverside lane opposite Servoz. 250m to the left is a bridge over the Diosaz giving access back to the village.

# 5:
# The Contamines-
# Montjoie Valley

*On the Roman Road above Notre-Dame-de-la-Gorge*

## Walk 25   Le Prarion from Bionnay

Routing: Bionnay – Col de la Forclaz – Le Prarion – Col de Voza –
           Bionnassay – Bionnay

Total ascent: 1019m (3343ft)

Timings: Bionnay to Le Prarion – 3½ hours
            Le Prarion to Bionnay – 2½ hours

Meals, snacks, drinks and accommodation available at Hôtel du
Prarion, Col de Voza and Bionnassay (accom. only).

Le Prarion is the summit of a major spur thrust down between the
Chamonix and Contamines-Montjoie valleys. This high finger of
steep, afforested land forces the River Arve, railway and Autoroute
Blanche into a 180deg. swing through gorges before reaching Le
Fayet and the Sallanches plain. Because it is surrounded by lower
ground, Le Prarion is an exceptional viewpoint in clear conditions,
rivalling Mont Joly to the south-west (Walk 27), though considerably
easier to climb! Its isolated position at the bottom end of the
Chamonix valley and 1000m (3300ft) directly above Les Houches
endows it with very special qualities as a vantage point.

The way up from the Contamines-Montjoie side is largely on
tracks serving the many chalets which dot the hillsides above St.
Gervais-les-Bains, but from Col de la Forclaz you are on a true
mountain path which gets quite exciting towards the precipitous
summit ridge. Easier ground lies ahead, with refreshment points and
a final walk down mountain roads back to the start.

**Bionnay**, where this walk begins, is a sleepy village just off the
D902, 3km south of St. Gervais-les-Bains. In July 1892, a
catastrophic mudslide emanating from the Bionnassay Glacier swept
down the steep-sided valley below and engulfed Bionnay, killing
some 200 people.

There is limited car parking space and care is needed not to block
access or disrupt traffic. Take the metalled lane (Route de
Bionnassay) to the left of the little chapel and after the first hairpin
bend, turn left on a wooded path called 'Chemin du Rocher' and
signed 'Montivon'. This climbs determinedly through forest with a
few gradient-easing bends to **Montivon**. Turn left into the hamlet,
then right at a water trough and left up past a house on a narrow path
signed 'Tramway du Mont Blanc' (NOTE: Walkers wishing to start
from Le Fayet or St. Gervais could catch the tram up to here. First
tram up 9am, 1st July to 7th Sept.).

The path continues steeply up and over the tramway. Keep ahead,

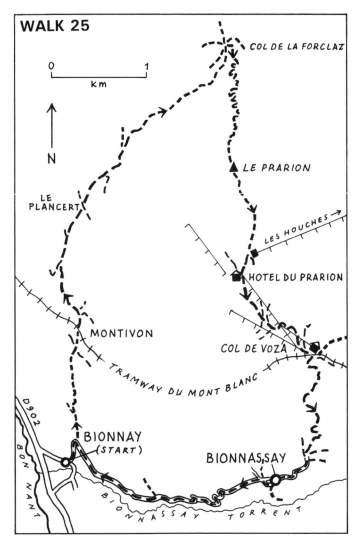

**WALK 25**

0 ———— 1
km

N

COL DE LA FORCLAZ

LE PRARION

LES HOUCHES →

LE PLANCERT

HOTEL DU PRARION

MONTIVON

COL DE VOZA

TRAMWAY DU MONT BLANC

D902

BON NANT

BIONNAY
(START)

BIONNASSAY

BIONNASSAY TORRENT

*View south-west from Le Prarion ridge*

ignoring a grassy track off right, and having passed chalets at Champlet descend on an improving track beneath high-tension electricity lines. Just beyond the next buildings, keep straight on, leaving the Chemin de Champlet and taking the Chemin du Plancert, waymarked 'Le Plancert and Le Prarion'. (The left turn descends sharply to St. Gervais.)

Now on a gently rising jeep track, the route reaches Le Plan. Ignore a muddy turning left, instead passing once again beneath the high-tension cables to arrive at Le Plancert and a track intersection. Keep straight ahead here, up through woods and out over open pasture, with increasingly fine views left (north-west) down to Sallanches and across to the imposing profile of the Desert de Platé (see Walk 24).

Keep forward off a hairpin bend (waymarked Col de La Forclaz) and enter mature woodland, still on a good jeep track which now contours on level ground. Just beyond a small cascade crossed by an ancient log bridge, stay on the good path (ignoring a turning left to Le Pontet and Montfort) which contours round in well established pine forest to **Col de la Forclaz** (1532m – 5026ft).

The col is a broad, earthy saddle, partly cleared of trees. Turn right (south) towards Le Prarion, henceforward waymarked with red

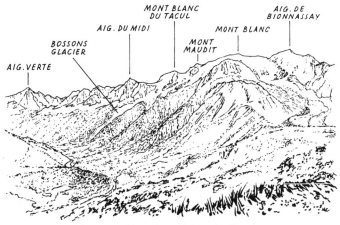

AIG.VERTE · BOSSONS GLACIER · AIG. DU MIDI · MONT BLANC DU TACUL · MONT MAUDIT · MONT BLANC · AIG. DE BIONNASSAY

*The Mont Blanc Massif from Le Prarion*

paint flashes. At first you follow a cleared forestry track, but soon the way is indicated left and becomes a path. (Further forestry activity here may affect this short section in future.)

Winding cunningly in zig-zags, the path wends a tortuous course up through dense, luxuriant woodland. There are a few scrambly steps to negotiate as you tackle the knobbly and vegetated northern end of the Prarion ridge, the summit of which is never for a moment in sight to spur you on! A fixed cable near the top adds security to a particularly exposed stretch, but it is without difficulty and soon **Le Prarion** is reached (1969m – 6460ft).

Though of moderate height only, this rocky summit with its little trig. point rises from surroundings which, on three sides, are of very low elevation. The result is a much sharper sensation of altitude than one would expect. The panorama is 360deg. in scope and renowned for its grandeur. Mont Blanc lies to the south-east above the Taconnaz Glacier, the Aiguille du Midi is poised above the Bossons Glacier, while farther east the Aiguille d'Argentière marks the extremity of the Chamonix valley at the Swiss frontier. To the north-east too is Col de Balme and the Aiguilles Rouges, north lie the Rochers des Fiz and Desert de Platé beyond the wooded Tête Noire. To the north-west, the Sallanches plain gives way to foothills, while in the south-west and south Mont Joly, Mont Tondu and the Dômes de Miage lead round to Mont Blanc.

Our onward route follows the ridge south, keeping left at the

163

bottom of a rocky slope then undulating pleasantly through low trees and banks of alpenrose to the top station of the cabin-lift from Les Houches. Blue-yellow waymarks lead on over easy slopes, increasingly popular with winter skiers, to the **Hôtel du Prarion** (1853m – 6079ft; privately owned; 30 places; permanently open; meals, snacks and drinks; nearby viewing table.)

Walk on south down the broad track which veers south-east past various junctions left and right and under ski-lifts to bring you to **Col de Voza** (1653m – 5423ft). The large, privately owned hotel has 50 beds, is open all year round and provides meals, snacks and drinks. There is a Tramway du Mont Blanc halt here and walkers wishing either to return to St. Gervais/Le Fayet or to Montivon near the start of this walk, could ride down if circumstances dictate. (Last tram down 5.30pm, 1st July to 7th Sept.)

Cross the tramway and start descending on a good jeep track, past a hostel with camping, and past car parking spaces. To the east rises the Dôme de Goûter above the Bionnassay Glacier. You soon join a metalled road which takes you down to the picturesque hamlet of **Bionnassay** (1350m – 4429ft). There is a Gîte d'étape, privately run, with 45 places. Reservations tel: (50) 78.28.63.

From Col de Voza you have been on the GR5 long-distance trail, but this now diverts towards Les Contamines and Col du Bonhomme (see Walk 31). Where it forks down left past a tiny chapel, turn right instead through the hamlet, then left. The narrow mountain road drops past La Fontaine settlement, round hairpin bends above the Bionnassay torrent, draining from the glacier of the same name. At the final sharp left bend, the outward route began and it only remains to walk downhill for 300m to Bionnay.

## Walk 26  Col de Tricot

Routing: Le Champel – Chalet de l'Are – Col de Tricot – Refuge de
　　　　Miage – Le Champel

Total ascent: 910m (2986ft)

Timings: Le Champel to Chalet de l'Are – 2¼ hours
　　　　Chalet de l'Are to Col de Tricot – 1¼ hours
　　　　Col de Tricot to the Miage Refuge – 1¼ hours
　　　　Miage Refuge to Le Champel – 1¼ hours

Meals, snacks, drinks and accommodation available at the Miage Refuge

*Special note: Although there is a footbridge during the summer months, extra vigilance is advised in the vicinity of the torrent issuing from the Bionnassay Glacier, especially in wet weather. Very early in*

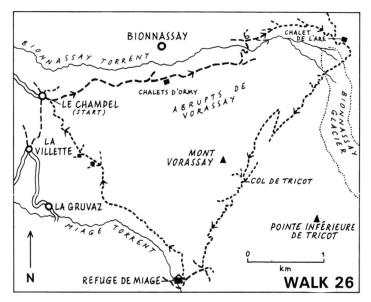

the season (May/early June), the bridge may not have been installed
and there is serious risk of avalanche.

This walk has great variety, and during July and August is enhanced
by wild flowers and shrubs, including the Martagon Lily and
rhododendrons on the col's approaches. There are, too, some
memorable views, especially of the Aiguille de Bionnassay and
Dômes de Miage. By following the Bionnassay torrent on the ascent,
and the Miage torrent for much of the return leg, Col de Tricot
becomes the high point midway on the walk.

**Le Champel** lies 2km up a twisting mountain road south-west of
Bionnay, itself some 3km south of St. Gervais-les-Bains. There is
limited parking space, so care is needed not to block access or traffic
flow.

Waymarked white-red-white at first (part of the Tour du Mont
Blanc routing), the broad track leaves east from Le Champel hamlet,
above meadows but soon enters larch forest. Fork right at a
junction (the TMB goes left), pass the Chalets d'Ormy and continue
on the gently climbing track, in and out of forest beneath the

'Abrupts de Vorassay'. Just before the Chalets du Chalère, turn left and cross the Bionnassay torrent on the Pont des Places. In 200m, turn right at a small reservoir and continue in an easterly direction, past Sur les Maures chalets and ignoring turnings off left and right.

Steep wooded slopes lead up right, to the Bionnassay Glacier, and you are soon joined by a path from the left (from Le Planet and Les Bettières) for the last steeper zig-zags up to **Chalet de l'Are**. A Tour du Mont Blanc variant from Col de Voza comes in here from the left, and its familiar red and white waymarks will be in evidence all the way to the Miage Refuge.

Swinging round south-west, our route drops to the terminal moraine of the glacier – here a rather dismal area of grey rocks and debris – and crosses the torrent on a metal footbridge. A sharp ascent brings you out into the magnificent sweep of **Combe des Juments**, with its colourful mid-summer rhododendrons and other alpine flora. During this ascent, the Aiguille de Bionnassay has soared above to the south-east.

Small streams and the Tricot chalet ruins are passed before the trail takes a big bend up Combe de Tricot and straightforwardly reaches **Col de Tricot** (2120m – 6955ft), a saddle between Mont Vorassay to the north-west (an easy 20min detour) and Pointe Inferieure de Tricot to the east. From this marvellous spot there is an exceptionally fine view of the Dômes de Miage's north face.

On its south-west side, the col is much steeper and there are many zig-zags to descend before reaching the Miage torrent valley visible below. A track finally leads to the **Miage Refuge** (1559m – 5115ft; privately owned; 30 places; guardian during the summer, closed in winter; reservations tel: 78. 13. 92; meals, snacks and drinks.)

From the refuge, walk north on a path past a calvary to the right. This contours north-west along steep mountainsides above the Gruvaz gorge and several torrent beds are crossed. Rounding a wooded corner, the way begins to drop gently past Les Lanches and Le Tranchet chalets, back down to Le Champel – a long but easy return stage.

### Walk 27   Mont Joly
Routing: La Chapelle – Porcherey – Mont Géroux – Mont Joly – Colombaz – Le Baptieu – La Chapelle
Total ascent: 1468m (4816ft)
Timings: Ascent – 4½ to 5 hours
Descent – 3 hours
Snacks, drinks and accommodation available off route at the

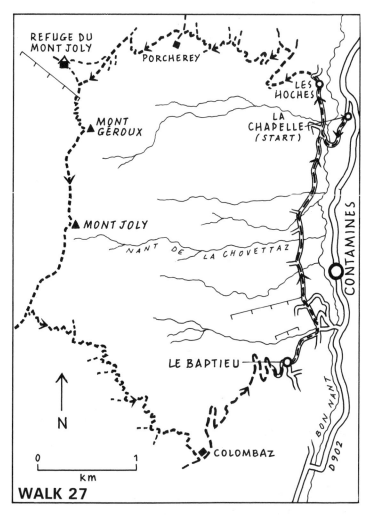

Refuge-Pavillon du Mont Joly.
*Special note: The summit of Mont Joly is best reached in good visibility, not only because it offers the best views in this region of all the major massifs, but also because its precipitous eastern flanks and*

*Mont Joly*

*summit topography make it potentially dangerous in mist, rain or high winds. Once on the main ridge, there are no escape routes except continuing ahead or turning back. Early in the summer, snow may still be lying in places and an ice-axe will provide additional security. It is advisable to obtain a weather forecast before setting out and to take along appropriate gear and energy rations for a climb of this nature.*

Mont Joly is the highest top on a lofty ridge curving south from Mont d'Arbois to Aiguille Croche and separated from the main glaciated peaks of the Mont Blanc massif by the Contamines-Montjoie valley. It tends to receive less snowfall, height for height, than the giants farther east, yet is no less challenging an objective for the fit mountain walker. Indeed, the altitude gain on this ascent is bigger than most in this guidebook, though the rewards are correspondingly rich.

Because it is set apart, Mont Joly is considered by many to rank as one of the great viewpoints of Mont Blanc and its neighbouring summits. However, the view also takes in a dazzling panorama of peaks in a 360deg. sweep around the horizon.

From across the Contamines-Montjoie valley, Mont Joly's grey flanks look high and treacherous, heavily eroded by watercourses and certainly offering no direct line to its summit. Instead, the ascent gains the ridge line farther north and lower down. By no means all the terrain is rocky, even some of the higher ground being grass covered, although the actual traverse of Mont Géroux and Mont Joly is rugged and steep in places. To the west of the ridge lies more hospitable country, for many years a winter skiing location and generously provided with lifts and access tracks.

The walk begins at **La Chapelle** (car parking space), a hamlet 2½km north of Les Contamines. Follow the lane south and over the Bon Nant river, then turn right (north) down to Les Hoches. Shortly beyond the hairpin bend over the steep-sided Nant des Meuriers stream valley, take a path left (waymarked green), up through trees, climbing at first steadily alongside the stream before swinging right (north-east) to houses and a mountain road at **Le Carteyron**. In about 150m, turn up left off the road on a track, and after a similar distance again, turn left (south-west) at Le Planey.

The way is now clear (waymarked red), twisting and climbing over meadow and through forest, past the occasional chalet and turnings off left and right; about half-way up you pass beneath high tension electricity lines. At the top edge of forest, cross the track leading to the cluster of buildings at **Porcherey** to your left, and continue ahead, climbing more straightforwardly now in a generally south-west direction and aiming for three chalets on the skyline. The track zig-zags up to pass them, then rises to meet the main ridge line coming from Mont d'Arbois. (Ignore paths off to the south). Approximately 400m down to the north-west stands the **Refuge-Pavillon du Mont Joly** (2002m – 6568ft. guardian during the summer; snacks, drinks and accommodation).

The ridge continues south, the path itself (waymarked blue/ yellow) passing a ski-lift and becoming appreciably steeper as it zig-zags above the precipitous slopes of **Mont Géroux**, passing a little west of the summit (2288m – 7506ft). For a while now the gradient eases off, with the bulk of **Mont Joly** rearing ahead. Soon gradient and terrain grow distinctly less friendly and the final 200m (650ft) are quite tough going, coming as they do at the end of a substantial ascent. Towards the top, take a direct line for the cairn and viewing table (though a flanking path does lead west of and behind the summit). Height 2525m (8284ft).

This will be the moment you have been waiting for and hopefully visibility will be good. For laid out before you at various distances around the horizon are the Diablerets mountains in Switzerland (east); Mont Buet and the Aiguilles Rouges (north-east); to the north and north-west the Aravis and Chablais; farther south-west and south the Vanoise and distant Oisans; and nearer at hand the peaks of Beaufortain. Whatever else is identifiable, it is impossible to mistake the great snowy massif of Mont Blanc itself, lying due east.

The summit ridge of Mont Joly is cleft by a sizeable hiatus, from the top of which rises Nant de la Chovettaz, one of a series of torrents draining down the steep, striated east face. The path (still requiring care, especially when snow is lying) passes this obstacle to the right (west) and follows the ridge down south to easier ground.

About 200m before the cairn on **Tête de la Combaz** (the next minor top), watch for a path off left (south-east), possibly over easy-angled snow at first. After initial zig-zags, it runs clearly down grassy slopes to La Combaz chalet and reaches steeper ground at the side of a stream valley (Ruisseau de Ty). Stay on the descending zig-zags, ignoring paths off left and right, pass a couple of ruined chalets and reach a jeep track at **Colombaz**.

Here the route turns left and follows the track over the Roget torrent and down hairpin bends (short-cut path) to the hamlet of **Le Baptieu**. Turn left at the chapel and left again down at the next road. On your right is the **Nivorin** Gîte d'étape and lightweight camping site, with **Les Contamines** town just across the Bon Nant river. The country road now leads pleasantly north and gently downhill through several hamlets, back to the turning right for La Chapelle. This final stretch is on the Tour du Mont Blanc and GR5 long-distance trails and gives good valley views of mountains to the east.

### Walk 28   The Tré-la-Tête Refuge and Lac d'Armancette

Routing:   Notre-Dame-de-la-Gorge – Cascade de Combe Noire – Tré-la-Tête Refuge – Chemin Claudius Bernard – Combe and Lac d'Armancette – Les Contamines – Notre-Dame-de-la-Gorge

Total ascent: 820m (2690ft)

Timings:   Notre-Dame-de-la-Gorge to Tré-la-Tête Refuge – 2¼ hours
Tré-la-Tête Refuge to Les Contamines – 2¼ hours
Les Contamines to Notre-Dame-de-la-Gorge – 1¼ hours
(A bus service operates between Les Contamines and Notre-Dame-de-la-Gorge up to 5pm)

Meals, snacks, drinks and accommodation available at the Tré-la-Tête Refuge and Les Contamines; refreshments at Notre-Dame-de-la-Gorge.

*Special note: This route is not recommended very early in the season (ie. springtime) or after storms, owing to the risk of avalanche and stonefall in Combe Noire and Combe d'Armancette. At other times, however, the route is quite safe. An ice-axe may be useful when crossing Combe d'Armancette before about the end of July.*

This fascinating itinerary combines features of historical interest with some unexpectedly wild and relatively unfrequented country, although the Tré-la-Tête Refuge itself is well patronised. Once the initial climb to the refuge has been accomplished, largely through forest, there is a fine traverse at around 1800m (5900ft) altitude on a well constructed path to Combe d'Armancette. Throughout this stretch, views down to the Contamines-Montjoie valley and across to the great striated buttresses of Mont Joly are stunningly beautiful.

Combe d'Armancette is crossed with care and followed by a descent past the diminutive Armancette lake (a worthwhile destination in its own right) to Les Contamines. The walk ends along the level valley floor, for the most part away from the motor road on a pleasant woodland track.

A surprisingly baroque building considering the setting, the chapel

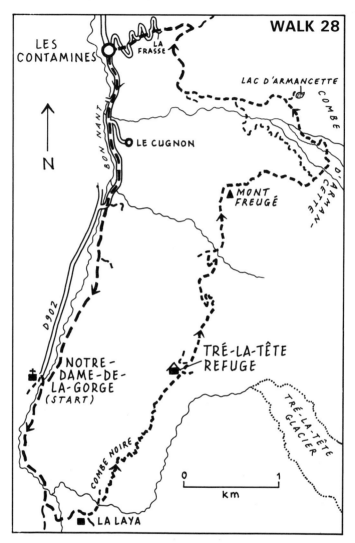

WALK 28

LES CONTAMINES
LA FRASSE
LAC D'ARMANCETTE
COMBE D'ARMAN-CETTE
N
BON NANT
LE CUGNON
MONT FREUGÉ
D 902
NOTRE-DAME-DE-LA-GORGE
(START)
TRÉ-LA-TÊTE REFUGE
TRÉ-LA-TÊTE GLACIER
COMBE NOIRE
0    1
km
LA LAYA

of **Notre-Dame-de-la-Gorge** is approached past a line of roadside shrines and is a place of pilgrimage, particularly on Assumption Day (August 15th). Its interior is typically Savoyard in character, with the exception of an Italian-Renaissance style altar-piece, and contains some interesting polychrome statues. As well as a bar/restaurant adjacent to the chapel, there is a large car park, for this is the start of a number of walking routes, as announced on a notice board just across the Bon Nant torrent.

Once over the bridge, turn right and walk up over the big rock slabs of the old **Roman road**, an ancient thoroughfare between Savoie and Italy's Val d'Aosta. Many a soldier once tramped its surface, but today's legions are all civilian, a mixture of strollers out for a picnic, walkers and mountaineers heading for wilder country at the valley head, and long-distance trekkers on the Tour du Mont Blanc or the GR5 Grand Traverse of the Alps.

The Roman road climbs through pine forest, passes a rock arch (Pont Naturel) off to the right, and crosses Pont de la Téna, a Roman bridge. About 200m after leaving the forest, take a track left signed 'La Laya, Cascade de Combe Noire and Tré-la-Tête'. Soon you cross the swift-flowing Bon Nant torrent on a wooden bridge and enter the recently inaugurated Contamines-Montjoie Nature Reserve.

The good track rises to chalets at La Laya, just beyond which take the path off left for Tré-la-Tête, noting the avalanche-prone slopes ahead. In 200m you come to a dramatic rocky cleft and the **Cascade de Combe Noire**. From the footbridge, the dizzy view down a vertical ravine to the torrent bed is an extraordinary sight. 10m farther on, turn up sharp right (straight on is a mid-height forest route to Les Contamines via La Sololieu ruins).

Held for a time within a little rocky valley, the path mounts avalanched slopes of displaced boulders and a chaos of tree trunks. Winding in and out past the stark columns of stripped trees, you are climbing over rock and tree roots for much of the time and the gradient is less kindly graded than most alpine paths. If you take a breather at a viewpoint, you can enjoy the prospect across the valley of Mont Joly's precipitous east face, riven by gullies falling from the summit ridge (see Walk 27).

Eventually the path reaches the flanks of Tête Noire and levels off, with the Tré-la-Tête Refuge visible ahead. The **Tré-la-Tête Glacier** has receded, leaving behind a vast expanse of grey, denuded rock down to the right in Combe Blanche. In a few minutes you reach the **Tré-la-Tête Refuge** (1970m – 6463ft. Privately owned; 100 places; guardian during Easter, Whitsun and summer periods; meals, snacks

*The Tré-la-Tête Refuge. Mont Joly right, Aiguille Croche left*

and drinks, drinking water outside; reservations tel: 47.01.68).

The refuge, it must be said, is not one of the region's most visually attractive and is surrounded by an unsightly scattering of pylons. However, its situation is unimpeachable, high above the Contamines-Montjoie valley and affording wide views in all directions. A glimpse of the Tré-la-Tête Glacier and the upper reaches of Combe Blanche is gained by climbing east above the refuge. (Onward from here lies the way up to the Conscrits Refuge (2730m – 8957ft), a more serious route in part over the glacier itself.) Also from this higher ground, the approaches to Col du Bonhomme are clearly visible (see Walk 31).

Continue north-east from the refuge and in about 50m take the right-hand upper path, waymarked Armancette and Contamines. This is the **Sentier Claudius Bernard**, a superbly constructed 'balcon' path sometimes just a ledge on steep mountainside but always good walking. Past a stone hut strongly reminiscent of a rural bus shelter, views ahead include the almost Dolomitic profiles of the Desert de Platé and Roches de Fiz (see Walks 24 and 23), rock scenery quite different from Mont Blanc and its snowy outliers.

The path descends in long stony zig-zags to a junction. Left drops

*Combe d'Armancette*

easily to Maison Forestière, Les Plans and thence to Le Cugnon – a good escape route or short-cut to the valley. Our itinerary, however, turns right, crosses the Nant des Fours stream and climbs gently, in and out of trees and past another 'bus shelter' before turning the corner of Mont Freugé and confronting for the first time the wild and desolate **Combe d'Armancette**.

Still 'en balcon', the path rises gradually, hugging close to rocky outcrops above high, vegetated cliffs. Emerging into the open, you drop to the edge of the combe and keep up right at the first stream (faintly waymarked 'Le Lac'). NOTE: Very early in the season there may be a risk of either avalanche or rock fall funnelling down from the cirque of rock faces and high glaciers above. At such times, exceptionally warm or wet weather will also increase the risks. If unsure about the wisdom of crossing the combe, drop left (north-west) on a zig-zag path which enters trees lower down, turns right to cross the Armancette torrent and rejoins the main route at a track below Lac d'Armancette.

You now walk out across rugged stony slopes on the intimidating sweep of Combe d'Armancette, beneath its soaring headwall of rock summits and unseen hanging glaciers. Occasional blue paint flashes indicate the best line, but much will depend on snow cover; fortunately this is easy-angled. Meltwater torrents are crossed either on snow or boulders and the quantity of rock debris lying around will be proof enough that this is no place to put up a tent!

Aim for the path continuation on more stable ground which zig-zags down, crosses a side-torrent and reaches a turning on the right to **Lac d'Armancette**. (At 1673m – 5489ft, it is only some 30m higher and 200m away – a pleasant spot for a break.). Below, the path widens to a stony track and passes the junction with the variant avoiding the combe, described above.

Continue downhill, cross a stream, pass a ruined chalet and arrive at an intersection by a shrine. Go on down the forestry track (the steep left branch is an uncomfortable short-cut!) and pass a junction right, to Chalets de Truc. You are now on the Tour du Mont Blanc routing as the track swings down left to rough car parking and the road end at **La Frasse**. Turn left and then proceed to short-cut all the road dog-leg bends on a good, well-walked track, right down towards **Les Contamines'** church spire. In the town are all shops, services and accommodation. A bus service to Notre-Dame-de-la-Gorge runs until 5pm.

Turn left along the main street and after about 2km (1 mile) keep ahead when the road bends right to cross the Bon Nant. This ancient

*Summer fête at Les Contamines, Col du Bonhomme distant left*

way on the river's meadowy east bank passes a variety of activity locations, including tennis, archery, horse-riding, rock-climbing and a campsite. It is a level, mostly wooded promenade leading out to the car park at Notre-Dame-de-la-Gorge.

**Walk 29   Col de la Fenêtre**

Routing:   Notre-Dame-de-la-Gorge – Chalet du Nant Borrant – Chalet-Restaurant de la Balme – Col de la Fenêtre – Les Prés Chalets – Chalet du Nant Borrant – Notre-Dame-de-la-Gorge

Total ascent: 1035m (3396ft)

Timings: Notre-Dame-de-la-Gorge to Chalet-Restaurant de la Bame – 1½ hours

La Balme to Col de la Fenêtre – 1¾ hours

Col de la Fenêtre to notre-Dame-de-la-Gorge – 2 hours

Meals, snacks, drinks and accommodation available at the Chalet du Nant Borrant, Chalet-Restaurant de la Balme and Notre-Dame-de-la-Gorge (no accom.)

*Special note: Very early in the summer (before early July) there may be snow cover on the final steep slopes to the col, when an ice-axe will be useful.*

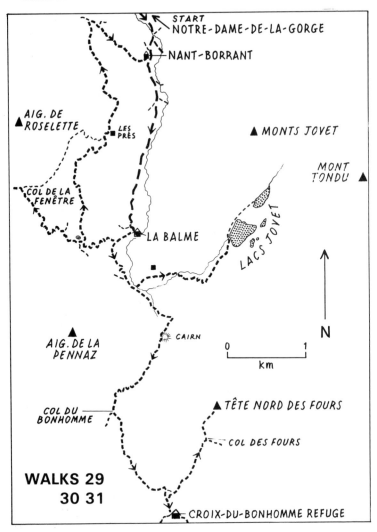

START
NOTRE-DAME-DE-LA-GORGE

NANT-BORRANT

▲ AIG. DE ROSELETTE

LES PRÉS

▲ MONTS JOVET

MONT TONDU ▲

COL DE LA FENÊTRE

▲ LA BALME

LACS JOVET

N

▲ AIG. DE LA PENNAZ

CAIRN

0                    1
km

COL DU BONHOMME

▲ TÊTE NORD DES FOURS

COL DES FOURS

**WALKS 29 30 31**

▲ CROIX-DU-BONHOMME REFUGE

The upper Contamines-Montjoie valley is tramped by many feet, for as well as leading to popular day-walk destinations, it is 'en route' for trekkers on the long-distance Tour du Mont Blanc and the GR5 Traverse of the Alps. It is therefore refreshing to note the recent establishment of the Contamines-Montjoie Nature Reserve to protect flora and fauna in this beautiful southernmost corner of the Chamonix area. Overnight lightweight camping, far from being banned, is permitted at two locations, thus avoiding indiscriminate pitching at unsuitable spots (much of the valley is farmland). Even litter is kept well under control by the provision and servicing of bins alongside the main track.

Col de la Fenêtre is one of three notches punctuating the lofty rock walls between Tête de la Cicle and Aiguille de Roselette, directly west of Chalet-Restaurant de la Balme. The ascent is not a difficult one (although the last few dozen metres are steep and rocky) and leads the walker through three kinds of terrain: a wide, pastoral valley floor, rugged stony mountainside with increasingly fine views as height is gained to the col, and high alps or pasture on a natural shelf above the tree line.

This walk (also Walks 28, 30 and 31) starts from the road-end car park at **Notre-Dame-de-la-Gorge**, south-east of Les Contamines. (For notes on the chapel and the Roman road, please turn back to Walk 28). Go up the Roman road, past the Pont Naturel (rock arch) off to the right, and cross Pont de la Téna, an ancient Roman bridge. Keep straight ahead and in 400m you will come to a clearing dominated by the Dômes de Miage and Tré-la-Tête Glacier up to the east, in which stands the **Chalet du Nant Borrant** (1460m – 4790ft; privately owned; 30 places; open during the summer months; meals, snacks and drinks. Reservations tel: (50) 47.03.57).

Beyond the Pont de Nant Borrant over the Lancher torrent (path down left to lightweight camping at La Giettaz) and a short climb, the track wanders through a broad, flat swath of pasture towards La Balme, visible ahead under the imposing rock and scree flanks of Aiguilles de la Pennaz (2688m – 8819ft). Farther up the valley and passing through a band of pine trees, you climb round a couple of bends and approach the **Chalet-Restaurant de la Balme** (1706m – 5597ft; privately owned; 80 places; open mid-June to end-Sept; meals, snacks and drinks. Reservations tel: (50) 47.03.54. Drinking water nearby and lightweight camping in the vicinity).

Just above the refuge (south-west), turn right, waymarked 'Col de la Fenêtre 1¾ hours'. Walking up the jeep track past an enormous

*North east from Plan de la Fenêtre - left to right:*
*Aig. du Goûter, Aig. de Bionnassay, Mont Blanc distant centre*

boulder on the right, you soon reach a track junction. Fork right (the way to the left is dangerous owning to rock-fall) and continue uphill on steady zig-zags past an old disused building in view beneath a rocky outcrop to the left.

At the next junction, turn right (signed 'Les Prés') – the left turn is again threatened by stone fall. Proceed on the track and at a waymark signpost by a small lake, take a path off left (towards Col de la Cicle and Col de la Fenêtre). You now follow the left flank of a small dry valley, then bear half-right over open pasture on a clear path. After two zig-zags, **Plan de la Fenêtre** is reached, a levelling off in the terrain where you may, perhaps, pause to take in the spectacular views back to the Mont Blanc massif, as well as gazing up at the rock barrier ahead. Col de la Fenêtre remains hidden and will not reveal itself until the final stages of the ascent.

A short way beyond a dismantled pylon base, bear left over a flat rocky area and possible snow patches on a cairned path (several alternative trods) which leads up left (north). A dramatic rocky (or snowy) scramble brings you up to **Col de la Fenêtre** (2245m – 7365ft). To the left of the saddle is a curious piece of abandoned ironware – the remains of an old E.D.F. pylon. Although views to the west are fascinating enough, they are eclipsed by the eastern prospect over Monts Jovet to the Tré-la-Tête Glacier and the high snows of Mont Blanc.

There is now a choice between two alternative routings to Les Prés chalets: either return to the small lake passed on the ascent and proceed on a good, clear track; or make your way first due east down to Plan de la Fenêtre, then north-east on an intermittent path over rough, undulating mountainside, finally dropping on bends to the chalets which stand at the top of forest.

The easier route to follow descends back to the small lake. Here turn left (north), following a substantial track up and down along a shelf of high pasture beneath Aiguille de Roselette (2384m – 7821ft), roughly parallel to some high-tension electricity lines which you pass under to descend to **Les Prés** chalets (1797m – 5896ft).

From here onwards, the way becomes a narrower path, winding round Les Rosières des Prés just above the tree line and to the east of the electricity lines. Having dropped to **La Chenalettaz**, turn right (south-east) downhill – not sharp right back along the hillside. Pass a path off left in 200m, then continue down, over two torrent beds and through forest to emerge at the Chalet du Nant Borrant. The outward route is now simply reversed back to Notre-Dame-de-la-Gorge.

### Walk 30   The Jovet Lakes
Routing: Notre-Dame-de-la-Gorge – Chalet-Restaurant de la Balme
          – Lacs Jovet. Return by same route.
Total ascent: 984m (3228ft)

Timings: Notre-Dame to La Balme – 1½ hours
            La Balme to the Jovet Lakes – 1¼ hours
            Descent to Notre-Dame – 2 hours

Meals, snacks, drinks and accommodation available at Chalet-Restaurant de la Balme and Notre-Dame-de-la-Gorge (no accom.) *Special note: This walk has a common start with Walks 28, 29 and 31. For route details between Notre-Dame-de-la-Gorge and Chalet-Restaurant de la Balme, please turn back to Walk 29.*

Because there is a well defined path throughout and gradients on the whole are not too demanding, this itinerary is suitable for walkers of all abilities; even adopting the steadiest of paces would not extend the walking day unduly. Nevertheless, close on 1000m of ascent is involved and there can be no doubt about it leading into splendid alpine surroundings with all the ingredients one would expect – a well-placed hut, beautiful flora, a mountain torrent, waterfalls, lakes and wide, airy views.

In their wild but accessible setting, the Jovet Lakes are well visited (there is trout fishing too – permit required), though much will depend on the time of your visit. Such is the scale of these mountains that a scattering of fellow walkers makes little visual impact.

Follow the well-walked path from the **Chalet-Restaurant de la Balme** which rises south-west and is waymarked Col du Bonhomme (see Walk 31). It climbs over rugged ground in front of the impressive flanks of Aiguilles de la Pennaz, veers south-east and grows steeper on stony zig-zags towards an electricity pylon. About 100m below it, turn left on a path waymarked 'Plan Jovet'. This crosses the Cascade de la Balme on a plank bridge, edges round the head of a ravine and climbs bushy slopes. Keep right at Mon Regard chalet to emerge on **Plan Jovet** at a large boulder and waymark sign to 'Lacs Jovet'.

To your right (south) will almost certainly be seen groups of walkers heading for Col du Bonhomme, on the long-distance Tour du Mont Blanc and GR5 treks; as we gain altitude, the col and its snowy approaches become progressively revealed.

Cross the torrent which issues from the **Jovet Lakes**, still far above, and walk up the path to its right. Gradually climbing east and away from the torrent, zig-zags are passed and a gentler gradient heads towards a lip of land with a waterfall to the left. Fully expecting this to lead immediately to the lakes, you may be forgiven a momentary disappointment as the route keeps you in suspense for a little longer, until finally a rise is topped and the first of the two main lakes lies

*Mont Joly from Nant Borrant*

ahead.

There is a magnificent backdrop of snow-streaked rock and scree rising to shapely Mont Tondu (3196m – 10,485ft) in the east, and the Monts Jovet to the west and north. Grassy levels in the foreground would offer fine prospects for wild camping pitches and it is possible to wander on along the lake's west shore, past an intervening knoll to the second, smaller, lake at 2194m (7198ft).

Turning back down the path, there is soon time and space to admire the view, especially over to Col du Bonhomme, bounded by the Aiguilles de la Pennaz and Tête Nord des Fours, and only some 160m (525ft) higher than where you are standing. Provided the waymark and boulder at Plan Jovet are watched for, the descent will be straightforward all the way down to Notre-Dame-de-la-Gorge.

### Walk 31   Col du Bonhomme and La Croix-du-Bonhomme Refuge

Routing: Notre-Dame-de-la-Gorge – Chalet-Restaurant de la Balme – Plan des Dames – Col du Bonhomme – Col de la Croix-du-Bonhomme and Refuge. Return by same route.

Total ascent: 1273m (4176ft)

Timing: Notre-Dame to La Balme – 1½ hours

La Balme to Col du Bonhomme – 2¼ hours
Col du Bonhomme to Croix-du-Bonhomme Refuge – 1 hour
Descent to Notre-Dame-de-la-Gorge – 3 hours

Meals, snacks, drinks and accommodation available at Chalet-Restaurant de la Balme, the Croix-du-Bonhomme Refuge and Notre-Dame (no accom.)

*Special note: Although nowhere difficult, this is a long and fairly strenuous walk requiring a good early start. It is advisable to obtain a weather forecast before setting out, as fine conditions will do much to increase your enjoyment of the high ground which can be bleak in wind and rain. From Plan des Dames onwards, there are usually snowfields to contend with and early in the season this can be a decisive influence on progress; an ice-axe may be useful. In any event, carry spare clothing and good sunglasses in addition to the usual gear appropriate to climbing to around 2500m (8200ft). This walk has a common start with Walks 28, 29 and 30. For route details between Notre-Dame-de-la-Gorge and Chalet-Restaurant de la Balme, please turn back to Walk 29.*

Following the coincident Tour du Mont Blanc and GR5 trails, this itinerary reaches a lofty and impressive location at the edge of Haute-Savoie Department. There is always the possibility of overnighting at the Croix-du-Bonhomme Refuge, transforming this into a 2-day expedition and, conditions permitting, enabling an ascent of Tête Nord des Fours or the Crête des Gittes ridge to be undertaken before returning to the valley.

The ascent from Notre-Dame-de-la-Gorge is a long and steady one and you will certainly not be alone on the trail! However, the La Balme hut is well positioned at the start of the serious climbing, while the Croix-du-Bonhomme Refuge awaits just beyond the highest point.

Follow the well-walked path from the **Chalet-Restaurant de la Balme** which rises south-west and is waymarked Col du Bonhomme. It climbs over rugged ground facing the impressive flanks of Aiguilles de la Pennaz, veers south-east and grows steeper on stony zig-zags, past a left turn to Plan Jovet and up towards an electricity pylon.

Once onto level ground, the way ahead is unequivocal, even in mist! It keeps to the right of a torrent (a feeder of the Bon Nant which runs right down the Contamines-Montjoie valley) and forks right at a concrete sluice. The thin trod diverging up right makes an apparently pointless climbing detour, but is useful when snowbanks slow down

*Hikers heading for La Balme Refuge and Col du Bonhomme -
Aigs. de la Pennaz top right*

progress on the main path.

After crossing a stream, the path climbs more steeply amidst alpine flowers and shrubs, up to a small plateau on which stands an enormous cairn. Legend has it that an 'English lady' and her companion lost their lives here during a violent storm; by adding a stone of your own to the already prodigious pile, you may ward off evil while remembering the tragedy.

From **Plan des Dames**, Col du Bonhomme is at last visible ahead, but in all probability there will be a sizeable snowfield to cross before reaching shaley slopes. Paths take both higher and lower lines – your choice will depend on conditions – joining forces to attack the final gravelly gullies which lead over more snow to the **Col du Bonhomme** (2329m – 8146ft).

Views south-west into Beaufortain include the Crête des Gittes ridge (an optional extension to this walk), while to the south-east lie Mont Pourri and the Tarentaise. Round to the north-east is

*Col du Bonhomme*

Tré-la-Tête and back down north the long Contamines-Montjoie valley stretches into the far distance. Nearer at hand to the left (east) is the double-headed rock called Bonhomme and la Bonne Femme.

There is a small hut right on the col offering shade in hot sunshine (lucky you!), shelter in wet, wind or cold. In fact, the col is a graceful saddle and an exciting situation to have reached, though in poor or threatening weather it can seem exceptionally bleak.

Turning left (south-east), take the rocky path which gradually slants up over rugged mountainside. There are likely to be more snow patches to cross, and small streams, one of which (Nant des Lotharets) is followed up to the tall cairn on **Col de la Croix-du-Bonhomme** (2483m – 8146ft; not technically the col, which lies 500m to the south, but a pre-war map inaccuracy which has stuck!)

This marvellous spot facing the mountains and valleys of Beaufortain is the walk's high point, but 10 min. away to the south will be seen the **Croix-du-Bonhomme Refuge** (Club Alpin Français; 40 places; guardian from mid-June to mid-Sept; 15 places in winter; limited meals and drinks – supplies are carried up daily from Les Chapieux! Water pipe outside; lightweight camping.)

Should an overnight stay be arranged (or a tent pitched in the vicinity), walkers could consider either of the following extensions before descending to the valley. Both require good weather.

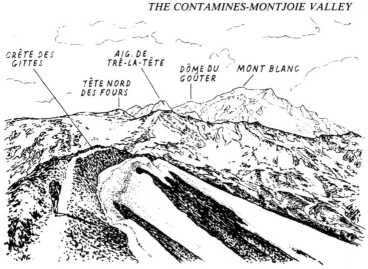

CRÊTE DES GITTES

AIG. DE TRÉ-LA-TÊTE

TÊTE NORD DES FOURS

DÔME DU GOÛTER

MONT BLANC

*View north-east from the Crête des Gittes*

**a) Crête des Gittes**: From the refuge, take the path a little west of south which clearly leads to the foot of this exciting ridge. After a narrow, rather exposed start, the way is securely cut into rock (engineered by mountain troops earlier this century) and winds airily from one side of the crest to the other. This is sensational walking of the highest quality! A leisurely hour each way is needed to traverse the entire ridge, but reaching the summit about half-way (2538m – 8327ft) and returning is enough to experience this unique feature. Early in the summer when snowbanks might still cover the trail, it can be safer to walk along the ridge crest itself, though great care and ice-axe safeguarding are obvious requirements. Allow 1 hour for the return trip.

**b) Tête Nord des Fours**: The path (a Tour du Mont Blanc variant) leaves north-east from Col de la Croix-du-Bonhomme and is likely to be snow-covered in part even in August; an ice-axe may be useful. You pass to the left of a ruined fortification and under high-tension electricity lines, continuing on over easy rocks or snow to **Col des Fours** (2665m – 8743ft).

Here the Tour du Mont Blanc routing descends to the east, but by following the ridge line roughly north, a straightforward ascent can be made to Têtê Nord des Fours (2756m – 9042ft). It is one of the

187

finest viewpoints over the northern Mont Blanc massif and was first visited by the Genevan naturalist Horace Bénédict de Saussure and his guide Pierre Balmat in 1781. The 'table d'orientation' will aid identification of features in the vast panorama. Allow 2 hours for the return trip.

To descend to Notre-Dame-de-la-Gorge, simply reverse the ascent route.

## Suggested shorter walks in the Contamines-Montjoie area
### REFUGE DU TRUC
Total ascent: 457m (1499ft) – 2½ hours' walking

A twisting road climbs east from Les Contamines-Montjoie to La Frasse, where there is car parking. The following itinerary is on the routing of the Tour du Mont Blanc long-distance trail and is waymarked red and white. Walk east up a broad jeep track, once used by mules and packhorses. Keep left where a track (from Lac d'Armancette) comes down from the right and pass two barns – Les Granges de la Frasse. After veering round left to cross a combe, you come close to a Touring Club Français 'point de vue' at 1512m (4961ft). Thereafter, the way is in forest for some time and passes a junction left to La Gruvaz. After more ascent, trees are left behind and you emerge over pasture to chalets and the Refuge du Truc (1720m – 5643ft; privately owned; 30 places; guardian from mid-June to end-Sept; closed in winter; meals and drinks.)

'Truc' means rounded summit and certainly the grassy top of Mont Truc fits the description. There is a fine panorama to the east, of the Dômes de Miage and its fringe of glaciers as well as the Aiguille de Bionnassay and Arête de Tricot. Return is by the same route.

### REFUGE DE TRÉ-LA-TÊTE
Total ascent: 780m (2559ft) – 3½ hours' walking

This walk starts from Le Cugnon, 1km south of Les Contamines-Montjoie, and takes the path heading south into forest from the top houses of the hamlet. After rising in zig-zags, the Nant des Fours stream gully is crossed and a left turn is made onto another series of zig-zags up to a path junction. Here go right, still ascending but emerging above the treeline. More twists and turns lead past a 'Maison Forestière' and a slight descent, before open mountainside is regained for the final climb to the Tré-la-Tête Refuge (for details please see Walk 28).

To return, walk north-east on the level 'Chemin Claudius Bernard', a well constructed path contouring high above the valley.

A wayside shelter is passed, then a drop on big zig-zags leads to a path junction by the Nant des Fours. Turn down left and in 300m turn right by the Maison Forestière and the Grande Combe stream. From here, the descent to Le Cugnon simply reverses the upward route.

## COL DU JOLY
Total ascent: 520m (1706ft) – 3 hours' walking

A jeep track (well used) runs up from between Le Baptieu and Le Lay (1km south-west of Les Contamines) to Les Tappes restaurant and entertainment complex. The Montjoie cabin-lift also provides access to this point, the start of this route. (If walking up from Le Lay, add 1 hour).

Walk towards the 'Village Savoyard' of Pré Revenaz (worth a look) but keep above it on a good track in and out of forest and parallel to the 'Signal cabin-lift. A sweeping right bend from Montjoie brings you up to the ridge crest, whereafter the views in all directions improve dramatically.

At the Signal buvette, keep right on the main track which contours round the Nant Rouge valley head, under two ski-lifts and not far from the small Lac de Roselette on the right, to arrive at Col du Joly (1990m – 6529ft). On the west side of the col, track become tarmac road making its tortuous way down to the departmental town of Beaufort. Return is by the same route.

*Trumpet Gentian*

# THE MAIN SUMMER-SEASON LIFTS

## (and operating times where available)

*Le Tour to Chalets de Charamillon and Col de Balme* – cabin-lift 8.30am to 12 noon; 2 to 5.30pm during the season.

*Argentière to Croix-de-Lognan and Les Grands-Montets* – cable-car daily from end-June to beginning September.

*Les Praz de Chamonix to La Flégère* – cable-car July and August 7.30am to 5.30pm; June and Sept. 8am to 5pm.

*La Flégère to l'Index* – cabin-lift: same times as La Flégère cable-car.

*Chamonix to Montenvers/Mer de Glace* – rack-and-pinion railway June and Sept. 8.30am to 5.30pm; July and August 8am to 6pm.

*Chamonix to Planpraz* – cabin-lift June and Sept. 8.45am to 12 noon; 1 to 5pm. July and August 7.30am to 6pm.

*Planpraz to Le Brévent* – cable-car; same times as Planpraz cabin-lift. (NOTE: The Brévent cable-car has been out of service for refurbishment work – check new operating schedules.)

*Chamonix to Plan de l'Aiguille and Aiguille du Midi* – cable-car (possible continuation by cabin-lift across to Italy) June and Sept. 8am to 5pm; July and August 6am to 5pm.

*Le Mont to Chalet du Glacier des Bossons* – chair-lift 9am to 12 noon; 2 to 6.30pm during the season.

*Les Houches to Bellevue* – cable car 8am to 12 noon; 1.30 to 6pm during the season.

*Les Houches to Le Prarion* – cabin-lift 9am to 12 noon; 1.30 to 5.45pm during the season.

*Le Fayet to Le Nid d'Aigle* – Tramway du Mont Blanc, calling at St. Gervais, Montivon, Col de Voza and Bellevue. Beginning of July to beginning of September – journeys up 9am to 4pm; journeys down 10.20am to 5.15pm.

(These times are accurate when going to press but are subject to alteration by the operators.)

*Alpine Pansy*

# USEFUL ADDRESSES AND INFORMATION

*Mountain Rescue* – Place du Mont Blanc, Chamonix, tel: (50)53.16.89.

Also St. Gervais, tel: (50)78.10.81.

*Compagnie des Guides de Chamonix* (mountaineering and walking guides) – Maison de la Montagne, 74400 Chamonix, tel: (50)53.00.88.

*Association Independante des Guides du Mont Blanc* – 98, Impasse des Moulins, 74400 Chamonix, tel: (50) 53.27.05

*Compagnie des Guides de St. Gervais-Val Montjoie* – Bureau des Guides, St. Gervais, tel: (50)78.35.37.

*Club Alpin Français* – Chalet d'Accueil, Avenue Michel-Croz, 7440 Chamonix, tel: (50)53.16.03.

*Office National des Forêts* (forestry information) – Maison Forestière, 603 Avenue du Bouchet, 74400 Chamonix, tel: (50)53.13.63.

*Chamonix Alpine Museum* – La Residence Mont Blanc, 95 Avenue Michel-Croz, 74400 Chamonix, tel: (50)53.25.93. (Open every day June to mid-Sept; 2 to 5pm, plus 10am to noon if raining!)

*Reserve Naturelle des Aiguilles Rouges* – Interpretation Centre on Col des Montets, north of Argentière. Tel: (50)54.02.24. (Open every day June to mid-Sept; 10am to 12.30pm and 1.30pm to 5pm.)

*Mountain Museum* – Place de l'Eglise, Les Houches. (Open every day except Mon; 3 to 6.30pm only).

*Merlet Mountain Zoo* – near Coupeau hamlet north of Les Houches. Tel: (50)53.27.80.

*Société Alpes-Transports (SAT)* – 74190 Le Fayet, tel: (50)78.06.33 (Bus services in the Mont Blanc region).

*Chamonix-Bus* – tel: (50)53.05.55 (Bus service in the Chamonix valley)

For main *Tourist Offices*, see under 'ACCOMMODATION' introductory chapter.

*S.N.C.F. Chamonix* – tel: (50)66.50.50 (Rail information)

*Taxis*, Chamonix – tel: (50)53.13.94.

*Air Mont-Banc* – Sallanches, tel: (50)58.13.31 (Air circuits of Mont Blanc).

*Martagon Lily*

*PRINTED BY MARTINS OF BERWICK*